Ross Neil

Arabella Stuart

The Heir of Linne

Ross Neil

Arabella Stuart
The Heir of Linne

ISBN/EAN: 9783744760836

Printed in Europe, USA, Canada, Australia, Japan

Cover: Foto ©ninafisch / pixelio.de

More available books at **www.hansebooks.com**

ARABELLA STUART.

THE HEIR OF LINNE.

TASSO.

Plays

BY

ROSS NEIL,

AUTHOR OF
'LADY JANE GREY,' 'INEZ,' 'THE CID,' 'ELFINELLA,' ETC.

LONDON:
ELLIS AND WHITE, 29 NEW BOND STREET.
1879.

ARABELLA STUART.

PERSONS REPRESENTED.

KING JAMES THE FIRST.

ROBERT CECIL, EARL OF SALISBURY.

WILLIAM SEYMOUR, *in love with Arabella, afterwards married to her.*

SIR JAMES CROFT, *a Gentleman of the Court.*

HUGH CROMPTON, *a Servant to Arabella.*

A PHYSICIAN.

A SEA-CAPTAIN.

ARABELLA STUART, *Cousin to the King.*

COUNTESS OF SHREWSBURY, *Aunt to Arabella.*

Lords, Ladies, Gentlewomen attending on Arabella, Pages of the King, an Officer, a Peasant-Bride and her Father, Guards, Sailors, Warders, a Woman-Attendant waiting on Arabella in the Tower, &c.

The Scene is laid in and near London, except during the Fourth Act, when it is on board a ship at sea.

ARABELLA STUART.

ACT I.

SCENE I.

An Antechamber in Whitehall Palace.

The EARL OF SALISBURY *discovered, with the* COUNTESS OF SHREWSBURY. *Music heard at intervals from within.*

Lady Sh. I fear my lord of Salisbury will chide
My boldness that hath dared to call him forth
From the revels that he graces; yet I know
He grudges less to leave the dance by night
Than the council-board by day.
　　Sal.　　　　　　　'Tis true my minutes
Are seldom mine. Since for brief space they are,
I pray you to command them, and to say
What I may do to serve you.
　　Lady Sh.　　　　　O my lord,
You know without my telling—if indeed
'Tis sooth what I have heard, that this great day,

Marked out for joy, since chosen by the king
To magnify his son and royal hope
With the style of Prince of Wales—that such a day
Is o'er, and no grace shown to my poor niece,
Who would fare better were she but my niece,
And not King James's cousin.

Sal. What is here
Your meaning, madam, passes my poor wit.
Upon the Lady Arabella's head
The king hath poured his bounty with full hands,
And drawn occasion from this joyful time
To endow her with a royal revenue,
Making her fortunes equal with her birth.

Lady Sh. Is gold your only med'cine, gold your food
For ev'ry longing?

Sal. I have found it, madam,
The fare most welcome to the most of men,
Wherein I will not say they judge amiss—
A diet solid, generous, and rich,
And appetising even while it fills.

Lady Sh. But for a maiden's heart, sir, not enough.
You mock my niece with gold, while all she would
Is leave to love.

Sal. Leave that she hath conferred
Upon herself, 'twould seem.

Lady Sh. Leave then to wed
The man she loves and cannot cease to love,
To whom her troth is giv'n, and lacking whom

She droops and pines e'en as a rose in the dark
That starves for sunshine.
 Sal.   For what now she bears
She hath to thank herself, who let her choice
Outrun the king's permission, and dared lend
Her ear to vows of love he knew not of.
 Lady Sh. Alas! is love indeed a froward child,
As poets paint, that we can thrust him out
When he comes in unbid? You know, my lord,
Great princes have been suitors for my niece,
And she was well content the king to all
Should deal rejection, for her heart was free;
But unto William Seymour, when he wooed,
She listened, for she loved.
 Sal.   The more her blame,
And more her cause to praise a gracious king
Who, where he might have punished, seeks no further
Than to restrain the offence, and unto her,
And him that shared her fault, accords free pardon
With but submission for the price.
 Lady Sh.   O say
With but the breaking of her heart for price—
I tell you, sir, she loves.
 Sal.   And if she loves,
Others have loved and lived, and so will she.
         [*Music heard.*
Nay, list how gaily there they carry it—
Another dance begun, and 'mong them all
None brighter in apparel and in smiles

Than your fair niece, more like, I fear, to break
The hearts of us poor courtiers than her own.
You were not at the masque? 'tis pity much;
My Lady Arabella played the part
Of a river-nymph, and truly with such grace
That all our eyes were ravished; coral, pearls,
Shells, water-lilies, and what know I else,
So gallantly became her that it seemed
Nature had fashioned them express for her
And her adornment.   Will you not go in,
And see them dance? for, as I think, she wears
Her naiad garments still.

   Lady Sh.   I have no heart
To look upon mock mirth.   And if she smiles,
Will Robert Cecil say he never used
His face to hide his thoughts?

   Sal.   With Robert Cecil
Your ladyship is hard.

   Lady Sh.   O sir, 'tis you
Are hard with me, and hard with my poor niece,
To whom, not grudging life, why should you grudge
The sweets of life?   What is there that the king,
Or you that counsel him, should fear of harm
From a weak maiden?

   Sal.   From a maiden nought;
You say right well.

   Lady Sh.   But if she weds you think
That she shall be the mother of a race
That from King James's hand shall pluck the orb?

Are he and his indeed so weakly set?

Sal.   You speak of things unfit for me to treat;
But, madam, this I'll say, there have been kings
Would not have let a cousin live whose name
Had so been used against them as this lady's
Against my master.   The Arabella plot
Tastes in our mem'ry yet.

Lady Sh.   Was't fault of hers
That knaves and madmen, playing at a plot,
Dared take her name in their irrev'rent mouths?
No more than Heaven's fault when Heaven is called
To hear a perjured oath; she was as true
As they were false, and this the king doth know.

Sal.   This doth he know, and therefore 'tis she dwells
Not in the Tower, but princess-like at court
In the king's own palace.

Lady Sh.   And is borne about
With the court where'er it moves.   My lord, your Tower
Is not your only prison.

Sal.   This is scarce
The thankfulness that you should show the king
For having set your niece in the highest place,
Next to his royal consort and himself
And his own princely issue.

Lady Sh.   Sir, the place
Is hers of right, since after him and his
She is England's nearest heir—nay, some would say

Nearer than they, being born within the realm,
As he and his were not.
  Sal.   Ay, this was made
The plot's chief argument.
  Lady Sh.   I was too hot;
I pray you pardon me, and bear in mind
An orphan's advocate may be allowed
A little favour, and an orphan 'tis,
Albeit a princess, that I move you for.
  Sal. Hark there! you hear they bring the dance
      to end,
The last to-night belike. Ay, even so;
Now doth the music play the revellers out.
  Lady Sh. An orphan, sir, with none to take her part
But her dead mother's kinsfolk, since it seems
Those of the father's side are too high placed
For pitying a cousin.
  Sal.   In the king
She hath a friend sufficient for her needs,
As by his bounty of to-day is shown.
Madam, farewell; the revels now are done,
And I was bid attend his majesty
In his closet ere he slept.
  Lady Sh.   O yet a word——
  Sal. My duty to your ladyship.   [*Exit.*
  Lady Sh.   A fox
May be outwitted; so may he be too,
For more than fox he is not—neither he
Nor the wise king he serves, a king so full

Of wisdom that it froths from out his mouth.

Enter SEYMOUR.

Sey. My Lady Shrewsbury!

Lady Sh. Who calls? How now!
Seymour, thou foolish youth, hast thou forgot
The air of the court for thee is perilous?

Sey. What hath proved mortal to my peace already
Can do me no more hurt. O speak, what news?
You made your suit to Cecil—and he said?
Nay, nay, no need to tell.

Lady Sh. No need in truth;
For he who coins his master into gold
By selling peace to Spain, how should he help
The planting of a rival royal house
To cheapen his own wares?

Sey. O if they knew
How loathed by her and me is that word royal,
They would put off the armour of their fears.
And is this all your comfort?

Lady Sh. All—unless
You'd have me tell with what fair phrase he spake,
And how, in solemn self-applause, he stroked
His beard the way of the hair. Would you find comfort,
You must yourselves achieve it.

Sey. How?

Lady Sh. Why, wed
With no leave asked, and see if kings dare part
Whom God hath joined.

Sey.   To this I have urged her oft,
But found her heart so faint and full of fears
Mine failed me with mere pity.
   Lady Sh.   Urge again,
And in such desp'rate sort that she shall need
More daring to deny than to consent.
   Sey. Sure when she hears no other way is left——
O could I see her now! methinks my words
Should come so hot and burning from my heart
As to spread fire to all, fire that pent here
Must scorch my life away.
   Lady Sh.   To see her now!
'Twere hard, and yet—— The revels are at end,
And the guests parting, she past doubt returned
Unto her chamber; there have I the right
To enter at all times, though you at none.
Come then with me; I will go pay my duty
Unto my princess-niece before I sleep,
You sitting waiting in my coach the while
Beneath her casement.
   Sey.   Ay?
   Lady Sh.   The casement's low,
And the night dark, and I a friend within
To give you signal when the way is clear.
   Sey. O dearest lady, I shall owe you more
Than the world's debt to the all-bestowing sky.
     Lady Sh. Come, I will help your wooing. [*Aside.*]
        And perchance
Thus help to found a glorious race of kings

Whom England, now by her clumsy Scot bestrid,
Will joy to obey.

   Sey.   What say you there? O haste. [*Exeunt.*

SCENE II.

ARABELLA'S *Apartment in the Palace.*

Two Gentlewomen discovered at work. HUGH CROMPTON *sitting apart, reading.*

   1st Gen. Our lady tarries long.

   2nd Gen.   You might have known
They would dance late to-night.

   1st Gen.   Would I could be
Where I might see them dance! But I'll be sworn
None fairer than my lady 'mong them all;
And these hands helped to set her fairness off.

   2nd Gen. And these no less, so please you.

   1st Gen.   But 'twas I
Ruffled her skirt in fashion of a wave.

   2nd Gen. A wave that none had known to be a wave
But for the diamond drops I sewed it with.

   1st Gen. Nor then perchance but for the water-
        lilies
And coral on her head—and will you say
Her head was not my work? Good master Crompton,
Seemed not my lady's head-tire ravishing?

   Cromp. Why, well enough. Your art had pleased
        me more

Could it have only painted on her face
A little sunshine.

1st Gen.   Nay now, on my word,
Her face was full of smiles.

2nd Gen.   Indeed it seemed
Her care was quite forgot.

Cromp.   O foolish maids!
Who take as easily a smile for joy
As a little gauze for waves. Had you but served
My lady long as I, and learned by heart
The smile her childhood wore from morn to night,
You would know mock from real.

1st Gen.   Voices! hark!
And footsteps, yonder in the corridor;
My lady comes at last.

Cromp. [*Opening the door.*] Ay, she it is,
Escorted home by a whole heathen troop
Of river-gods and nymphs.

Enter ARABELLA, *with Lords and Ladies, all in masquerading dress.*

1st Lord.   Thus have we brought
Our royal naiad to her native grot,
And now must take our leave, wishing her dreams
As sweet as ever murmuring sea-shell soothed.

Ara. Most worthy Triton, and kind lady nymphs,
My thanks to all for this your courtesy,
And be your dreams as fair—of golden sands,
And mermaid-haunted palaces of pearl.

1st Lady. I would not dream of mermaids; I would dream
Of dancing, and your fish-tailed dames dance not.
  2nd Lord. They are unlucky too; they always come
To a bad end.
  1st Lord.   How so? Ha! now I see;
Good, very good.
  2nd Lady.   'Tis well for us we stand
Upon a better footing, as our prowess
In the dance to-night hath proved.
  1st Lady.   O what a night!
Good faith, so merry a night I ne'er yet knew.
  Ara. Nor I—a merry time, e'en as you say;
Feast, music, dance—why, there was nought that lacked.
What! will you go so soon?
  1st Lord.   Madam, I fear
You are overtired already.
  Ara.   Tired! not I—
I feel as far from sleep as though mine eyes
Had never known his power; but you shall go
And seek him if you will. Good-night to all
Brother and sister rivers, small and great.
  1st Lord. Good-night, dear lady; may our father Neptune
Have you in his safe keeping evermore.
  Ara. A guardian something cold—yet take my thanks.   [*Exeunt Lords and Ladies.*
What, girls! I have made you wait.

1st Gen. Think not of that.
Enough for us to see your ladyship
Returned so full of mirth.

Ara. Ay, full of mirth,
Only a little weary. [*Seating herself.*] Marvel not
To see me weep; 'tis nought but weariness.

1st Gen. Alas! how is't?

2nd Gen. Sweet mistress!

Cromp. O I knew.

Ara. And gladness to be back among my friends—
For friends you are, I feel, and I have been
Where all was show and seeming. Kind old Hugh,
Look not so grieved.

Cromp. Not if you will not weep.

Ara. I will not more; I have no cause—nay, rather
Cause to be glad. I bring you home good news;
The king, in honour of this joyful time,
Hath made me rich with a great revenue
Whereby you all shall profit; my friend Hugh
Shall feel my friendship, and my faithful maids
Have dowries when they wed—and wed they shall
Whene'er and whom they please. [*Knocking heard.*
Who knocks? Pray, first
A moment's breathing-space. So—open now.
CROMPTON *opens the door, and Enter* LADY SHREWSBURY.
What! my kind aunt?

Lady Sh. Forgive me that I come
So late a visitant, but I was fain
To see you ere you slept. Child, are you well?

Ara.   Seem I not well? I have danced and laughed all night
As water-sprite did never. See you not
I am a water-sprite? or must I sit
For ever by my fountain to be known?

Lady Sh.   I can divine a fountain near at hand
That hath not long been stopped. Beseech you, cousin,
Grant me a little of your private time.

Ara.   Good friends, you hear; pray pardon me awhile.

Lady Sh.   Sleep or whate'er you will, but come not back
Until your lady calls; 'twixt her and me
There's much to say.

                [*Exeunt* CROMPTON *and Gentlewomen.*

Ara.   What should there be to say?
Unless indeed that of all kinswomen
You are the kindest, I the thankfullest?

Lady Sh.   Is't true this day you built your hopes upon
Is past, and brought you from the king no grace
Saving a little gold rubbed on your palm?

Ara.   'Tis true the king hath been to me to-day
Most bounteous of his purse.

Lady Sh.   Ay, of his purse?
Not of your liberty?

Ara.   He hath not said
When I may have more liberty than now—
But will one day perchance.

Lady Sh.   And till that time
You are content to wait?
    Ara.   To be content,
Or strive to be, is the duty of us all.
But see, good aunt, your questions crowd so thick
That scarce they leave me room to say how much
Your presence glads me.
    Lady Sh.   To my mind content
Is a full stop that we should only write
When the greatest good is reached. Is that good
        yours?
    Ara. Who is too eager for more good may lose
The little that he hath. Can I, who seem
To some a creature worth the envying,.
Not be so much as patient?
    Lady Sh.   Cry you mercy;
I had forgot your palate must have changed
With your changed fare, since those old days you
        dwelt
Among your lowly kin of the mother's side.
Now I remember, and will turn my pity
To gratulation. Yea, to live at court,
To walk a princess next the king and queen,
To play a part, though but a wat'ry part,
In gauds like these, with gold enough in purse
To pay the reck'ning—this should be well worth
All else that life can show.
    Ara.   So some might think.
Alas! what have I done that thus you seek

SCENE II.]   *ARABELLA STUART.*   15

To make that harder which was hard before?
   Lady Sh. What! have I fetched forth tears? at least I see
It is with much ado you choke them down.
I knew I touched an easily bleeding place;
Where shall we find a salve? [*Throwing open a window.*
                      Hither, and try
What comfort lurks in the solemn midnight air.
You will not come? then shall it come to you,
And kiss your paling roses back to life.
Make ready now to see the sight in the world
That most you long for.
   Ara.   He! is't he?

   Enter SEYMOUR, *leaping in by the window.*

   Sey.   Yea, I,
Who have hungered till I starve. What! pale, my love?
And tears upon your cheek?
   Ara.   Regard them not;
Weeping is now no pain, for thou art by.
   Sey. I am glad that thou hast wept, since thus I see
That still thou lovest.
   Ara.   Hast thou doubted then?
I never doubted thee; to me thou wast
But as a missing part of mine own self—
Though missing O how long! And I forgot;
I should not joy to see thee, for my joy

Is paid for with thy peril. I am wrong
Even to wish thee near.
 Lady Sh.   Fear not for aught;
None knows of this, nor shall; the doors are locked,
And I, a trusty sentinel, on guard.
Drink your full fill of comfort till by me
You are told 'tis time to part.
  [*She seats herself by the window, seeming to take no
   further notice of the others.*
 Sey.   So thou wast jealous
To hear I doubted; if I doubted ever,
The fault was thine.
 Ara.   I know that now you speak
Only to vex me, yet will not be vexed
Where I should be so glad.
 Sey.   Were but thy love
As large as mine, we twain should now make one
In spite of kings and councillors and all.
Thou couldst not have denied.
 Ara.   If I denied,
'Twas that I dared no other. I perchance
Am weak, but not my love.
 Sey.   Then prove it yet,
By daring for my sake. Say thou but yea,
And all is done—the time, the place, the means,
Ready in my brain devised—a rev'rend man
To give us blessing found, whom I will bring,
Myself disguised, disguised unto thy room,
So thou but love me well enough to dare

For me, as I for thee.

Ara.   O but the king—
Thou know'st him not as I; he jests and laughs,
Yet when he hath a purpose keeps it still,
And the more stubbornly the more opposed,
As a knot that, strained at, tightens.

Sey.   Be it so;
But both our disobedience and our joys
Shall from the king be hid, and if at last
They come to light, 'twill cost him more to part
The husband and the wife than to divide
A pair of sighing lovers. But I see
Your measure of love suffices not for this.

Ara. Nay, were it less, I think I could dare more;
But being loved by thee and loving thee
Is unto me so full a happiness,
So new and strange and sweet, that miser-like
I have more fear to lose than hope to gain.
May I not shelter in content awhile
Ere wand'ring forth anew?

Sey.   Ay, you can gild
Your coldness with fair words. I know how 'tis;
Born royal, you would fain be royal still.

Ara. O that there were a way to drain my veins
Of whatsoe'er may flow therein of royal,
And leave me but well-born enough for you,
I'd kiss the knife that bled me. To be royal,
This is the spectre that hath ever stepped
'Twixt me and what I would; 'must,' and 'must not,'

And 'royal,' were the words that first I learned.
Since I was born I have been as one who stood
On a grey shore where mists and rain-clouds lay,
While white-sailed ships, winged for some happy realm,
Gleamed in far distant sunshine out at sea.
And can you think I would not willingly
Cast off my royalty?—as willingly
As this bespangled trash it decks me with.

  Sey. To cast it off is yours if so you will;
Be royal no more, but William Seymour's wife.

    Ara. Can men cast off their fate because they
        would?
And policy and state necessity,
These are my fate, and had you felt as I
How straitly they can curb, with a hand how hard,
You would own their power, and fear.

  Sey.   Fate is a word
That sluggards use, to excuse their sluggishness,
While the braver sort revolt, and oft-times find
What they called fate was but the hollow image
Of their own patience. Will you sacrifice
Upon that altar both yourself and me,
And years of love and joy that should be ours,
And not e'en once make trial of revolt?
Are you so much a slave?

    Ara.   And if revolt
Should make us doubly slaves? I am now but curbed,
And find it hard to bear; but punishment,
Thy punishment perchance, ruin of thy life,

That dawned so fair till crossed by me, its cloud—
O save me, Heav'n, from this!

 Sey.   Say not 'tis I
You are tender of; were I your only care
You would not be so wary.

 Ara.   Is it thus?
Why then, command me to whate'er you will.
In all things I obey.

 Sey.   Then I command
That thou shalt be my wife.

 Ara.   What I have said
I will not now unsay—if you are bent
To stake all hope upon a single throw.
I have lived long upon a little hope,
And so could still methinks, but with no hope
My spirit would droop to death, or to a deep
More dark if darker were. Nay, nay, frown not;
I'll keep my word.

 Sey.   Mine, all mine own, at last!

 Lady Sh. [*Coming forward.*] What! you have
  conquered? this is well, for time
No more to-night may serve you; one by one
I have seen the lights from ev'ry window fade
Till all the palace rests, or were at rest
Save for the sleepy porters at the gate
Waiting to let me forth; we must make haste,
Or drowsiness itself will rouse them up
To anger first, then wonder. Get you gone
The self-same way you entered, and lie hid

In my coach until I come. O never grudge
To say farewell; think that you next shall meet
Upon your wedding-day.

Sey.   So hath she sworn;
And she shall find in me a creditor
Exacting of fulfilment.

Ara.   I am but
A debtor over-willing.

Lady Sh.   Take a kiss
In earnest of full payment, and begone.

Sey. Farewell until I come in secret back
To claim my secret treasure hidden here;
I'll find the way full soon. Yet one kiss more
To live upon till then.

Ara.   Farewell; my prayers,
Happier than I, shall follow where thou goest.

Lady Sh. Away, away!

[*Exit* SEYMOUR, *by the window.*

              Good-night, thou royal bride,
And if thy royalty e'er shine more full,
Forget not me and all my service done.   [*Exit.*

Ara. O Heaven, thou that show'st me so much joy
As a promised land before me, shut it not
From out my view again, or kill me first.
Ne'er to have had was well, and I could bear,
But to have had and lose were black despair.

              [*The Curtain falls.*

END OF ACT I.

ACT II.

SCENE I.

A Room in Whitehall Palace.

SALISBURY *discovered, speaking with a Page.*

Page. My lord, I have delivered to the king
Your message punctually—that you were loth
To break upon his leisure——
   Sal.   Which I knew
No prince in the world e'er bought so dear as he,
With labour dedicate to his country's good—
You missed not that?
   Page.   Nay, nor aught else, my lord—
But that you were constrained to trespass now
By a matter nearly touching him, which craved
Instant consid'ring.
   Sal.   And to this he says?
   Page. That he will give his presence here forth-
      with.
And lo, he comes already.

Enter KING JAMES, *attended by Pages.*

   Sal.   As the sun
That breaks upon the cloud-perplexèd earth,

Good-morrow to your sacred majesty.
 King. Well, man, what would you? By my soul,
  I think
You all would stand without me as young babes
Without their nurse, so oft you tug my skirts
To save your stumbling; all one where I be,
Afield with the game in sight, or in the core
And midmost kernel of a syllogism,
You still must come to me and none but me
To keep you on your feet.
 Sal.   'Tis true indeed
That when our stores of wisdom are run dry
We are constrained to seek it at the fount.
 King. I wish you ne'er may drain the fount as
  well,
You bring your empty buckets there so oft.
 Sal. This might we fear, had we not learned by
  proof
It is a source perennial.
 King.   Ill for me
That e'er you found it so, since for that cause
You keep me chained in bonds as tight as those
That Aristæus bound wise Proteus with,
Hauling him forth from where *fessus ab undis*
Se recipit—your lordship's mem'ry serves?
 Sal. Ay, and I see your majesty will seek,
As Proteus did, to 'scape, with the oracle
Still undelivered—therefore will I haste
To unfold my bus'ness, but I pray you grant

Your royal ear in private.
  King.   Stand back all
Profanum vulgus; from the common gaze
The great affairs of kings and states—*arcana
Imperii*—must be wrapped up and hid.
  [*All retire to the back part of the stage, except the*
    KING *and* SALISBURY.
Well, gossip, well? what hath my little beagle
Nosed out for me to-day that he hath scratched
So hard to be let in?
  Sal.   Somewhat, so please you,
Touching your majesty's near kinswoman,
The Lady Arabella.
  King.   One we deemed
We had broken in—and doth she still curvet?
  Sal. But though both she and he that dared to
    woo
Seemed willing to forego where you forbade,
Yet in most wise distrust your majesty
Commanded me to set a secret watch
On her and all her dealings, and, as ever,
Your wisdom by the event is glorified,
For one whom in her household I had hired
Hath brought me tidings which, if worthy trust,
Show that the twain, abusing thanklessly
Our simple confidence, already stand
Bound in rebellious wedlock.
  King.   Wedlock! what!
Zounds, man! is that your word?

Sal. A word, my liege,
I fear too fit, for if what I have heard
Be not against all truth, the knot is tied.

King. So is the knot, ye loon, upon the rope
We'll whip them with, and you shall feel it too
For all your beagle's whine. Was't tied you said,
And bound? there spake you well; we'll find a cord
To bind them and to tie them up so hard
They shall not wag a finger; they shall feel
Wedlock is not the only yoke that is,
Nay, nor the heaviest, although, God wot,
Heavy enough; so the poor puling fools
Would find full soon, and, troth, I have a mind
To let them find, and never vex myself
Meddling with bridled ass or brided man,
Who truly do but stand an ell apart.

Sal. I see again, as oft I've seen before,
That wit and wisdom are twin sisters, born
To be the handmaids of your majesty.

King. And whom should wit best fit if not a king?
Should he not be in that and all things else
Facilè princeps?

Sal. As in sooth you are.
But, sire, beseech you, think how you will deal
In the bus'ness of this lady, which, most sure,
If she hath so revolted as 'tis said
And no curb found, is grave and full of peril
Both to your place and person.

King. On my word,

She is nought to me that I should put myself
In peril for her sake ; that is a sight
You ne'er need think to see.

 Sal.   And peril 'twere
Both to your royal self and royal heirs
If you should let another stock take root
And put forth leaves and branches, and with years
Grow to a stately tree in whose broad shade ·
Traitors might safely shelter, as we saw
Behind this lady's bare and branchless name
They sought to shelter once.

 King.   Ay, trust me well,
I've not forgot; of Arabella plots
I'll have no more.

 Sal.   Nor only here at home
The danger were ; for foreign states that now
In England see but you, and therefore pay
To you and England homage, then might deem
Their need of homage less, in England then
Seeing a house divided 'gainst itself
That through its own divisions might be ruled.

 King. Ay, ay, revolt at home, and wars abroad—
Here is fair recompense that she would make
To me that fed and warmed her at my hearth,
And pardoned her what traitors would have done
Against me in her name, and asked for all
Only obedience. But she soon shall find
Obedience I will have.

 Sal.   'Twere hard indeed

To let that wall of safety and of peace
Built by your wisdom round us be rent through
To give a pair of lovers room to kiss.

 King. I tell you, man, they ne'er shall kiss again,
If I am king, and king I am, albeit
Perchance they wish me less. Part them this day;
Here is the task I give you.

 Sal.   And a task
That shall be quickly done, if not to-day,
At least with no more of delay than serves
To make my knowledge of their treason sure;
For yet I have but hints and dark reports,
With here and there a piece of proof, too weak
For punishment to build on.

 King.   What! you hold
The clue in hand, and yet must take an age
To ravel out? if I had been so dull
I and my Lords and Commons all had made
Once on a time a journey in the air.

 Sal. Alas! my liege, this lady with her smiles
And honeyed words and ways hath so bewitched
Those nearest to her person that all arts
To unlock their lips were vain, so on our side,
To watch for us, are only varlets left,
The meanest in her household, and who stand
The lowest in her counsels.

 King.   Plague no more
Your old carle's pate for that, but make to-night
Your thanks to Heav'n for giving you a king

Who hath learned more than your grey hairs can
    teach
Of policy and statecraft.
    Sal.   So full oft
I have seen by proof.
    King.   Ay, and shall see again.
You fain would know if Arabella Stuart
Be William Seymour's wife? then know you shall,
Within this hour; and how? you next would ask—
That shall you learn with waiting.   [*To one of the
    Pages behind.*]   Hither, boy;
I have a charge for you. [*To* SALISBURY.] You wonder
    much
What way I'll go to work?
    Sal.   True, sire, I stand
In wonder lost, knowing of your counsels nought
But that great Heav'n hath put them in your heart.
    King. Sirrah, go give the Lady Arabella
Our cousin-like and princely commendations,
And tell her we entreat her here to lend
Her presence for a space.
    Page.   Not Mercury,
Despatched by Jove, might fleeter be than I
To do your royal bidding.   [*Exit.*
    King. [*To a second Page.*] You, lad, next;
Here is another charge. Go forth, and fetch
Such of my council as you chance to find
Within the palace precincts, unto whom
Say they are called to be our witnesses

In bus'ness of great weight—*magni momenti*—
Wherein we are now engaged.

 2nd Page.   As Heav'n's commands
Are sacred, so no less your majesty's.   [*Exit.*

 King. [*To a third Page.*] You, send some stout
  half-dozen of my guards
To seize within his lodging on the person
Of William Seymour, who, when seized, forthwith
Must be brought hither, near at hand to wait
Our royal pleasure, but to enter not
Until we give command.

 3rd Page.   I am but born
To do your high behests.   [*Exit.*

 King. [*To* SALISBURY.] You marvel still?
See where the lady comes.

       Enter ARABELLA.

         Ho! my fair coz,
I give you greeting. Now who is't you send
Your eyes in quest of? 'twas myself who spake,
And said, I give you greeting.

 Ara.   I the same
Unto your majesty.

 King.   How may this be?
You are pale, and by my troth as out of breath
As a new-caught hare.

 Ara.   Think you indeed, my liege?
Perchance because I made great haste to obey.

 King. I would have said 'twas fear, if I could guess

What cause of fear you had—and all effect
Argues precedent cause, as verily
Both Aristotle knows and the whipped dunce
That squeals to see the rod.
 Ara.   Fear, say you, sir?
What need should be for fear?
 King.   Certes, obedience
Is the cat that best may look a king in the face;
So you do well to smile, and might methinks
Smile boldlier yet than now. Still must I marvel
You have so little in you of the Eve
You come, and ask not wherefore you were called.
 Ara. And wherefore then, so please you?
 King.   Since I know
You are in love—what mean you starting thus?—
Knowing, I say, how much you are in love
With masques and plays and all that may divert,
I have bid you hither to be looker-on
At a *comœdia* or comedy
That we have now in hand. Are you so glad
That you can scarce believe?
 Ara.   Who were not glad
Being so favoured by your majesty?
Whom with my heart I thank.
 King.   No need, no need.
The subject's duty merits to be paid
With the favour of the prince, and by my soul
You please me well, in that you have shown yourself
Docile to discipline—as saith Cicero

Ad disciplinam docilis—and quenched
So wholly in your heart the foolish flame
That there had lit itself.
 Ara.   Ay, sir. I pray,
When will this play begin?
 King.   And you did well
And wisely so to obey, since still we see
Who tastes forbidden fruit must find it turn
To ashes in the mouth—forbidden whether
By kings or Heav'n. For truly, if you think,
You will discern the attributes of kings
To be the same as Heav'n's—at their good pleasure
To create or to destroy, to deal out life
Or death as fit may seem, to judge all men,
Being judged or held accountable by none,
And in each heart to have the foremost place
Of love and worship. What! you see how close
The likeness runs?
 Ara.   O you are great, I know—
And great is Heaven too. But, sir, the play—
When shall we see the play?
 King.   Soon—soon enough.
Lo yonder some invited witnesses
Who come to look; *spectatum veniunt.*

*Enter some Lords of the Council, making obeisance to
 the* KING.

My lords, good-morrow. You are here convened
To be the audience of a comedy

Briefly to be presented, but we wait
Some of the players yet.   Be seated all;
And you, fair cousin, in the place of honour
Here by my side; meantime I will expound
The plot or argument; and, as I think,
I can unwind a plot as well as most—
What says my lord of Salisbury?
  Ara.   So then?
  King. Our cousin hath scant patience.
  Ara.   Ay, because
I love to be diverted, as you say,
And ne'er was in such vein for mirth as now.
I hope the argument be merry enough;
Comedy was your word.
  King.   This then it is;
First you shall see appear a prisoner
Brought in by guards.
  Ara.   A prisoner—and guards—
Here's solemn matter.
  King.   Ay, a prisoner
Brought in by guards, to say his last farewell
To his new-wedded wife.
  Ara.   A sight to make
Good wives and husbands sad.   And then what
  comes?
  King. That shall you see yourself, since I discern
All that pertains is now in readiness.
What ho! let him that plays the prisoner
Make entrance and begin.

Enter SEYMOUR, *with Guards.*

         Mark where he comes,
And how so anxious-like and peeringly
His eyes rove to and fro to seek his wife—
For, as I said, the twain are now to part,
And 'tis a woesome thing without farewell
To part for ever.
 Ara.   O but I am here—
Love, husband, I am here.
  [*Rushing forward, and throwing herself into* SEY-
   MOUR'S *arms.*
 King.   So! have you heard?
Public confession made! She clean forgot
She did but sit spectator at a play.
 Sey. Hang not thy head; bid them defiance all
From thy safe fortress in thy husband's arms.
Yea, husband, sirs, I said—and she my wife,
My wife and chiefest glory.
 King.   What! again!
Confession on both sides, and made in presence
Of divers well-reputed witnesses.
Multorum oculis testatior.
[*To* SALISBURY.] Said I not? said I not?
 Sal.   The best device
Since Solomon gave judgment, worthy none
Save Israel's wise majesty and yours.
 King. I'm not so doited yet but I can spread
A net to catch a bird, or e'en maybe

A pair, as now. Come, good my lords, with me;
We'll leave them limed awhile, till we devise
A way to clip their wings.
   Ara. [*Throwing herself on her knees before the* KING.
                             Pity and pardon!
King, cousin, pardon, pardon. O have mercy!
   King. Guards, watch them still; we presently will send
Word of our pleasure, *voluntatis nostræ.*
Come, sirs, and when our bus'ness is despatched
I wish it may be supper-time, for, troth,
Not Solomon could keep his wit alive
Upon an empty stomach; empty stomachs
Are the vacuum by Nature most abhorred.
   [*Exeunt all but* SEYMOUR, ARABELLA, *and Guards,
      the latter remaining at the back part of the stage.*
  Ara. [*Still kneeling.*] O pardon, pardon!
  Sey.   Nay, abase thyself
No longer; he is gone, and heeds thee not.
   Ara. Gone—ay, 'tis so, and we twain left behind,
Pris'ners awaiting doom. O 'twas my fault,
Because I could but ask with parrot tongue
Mercy and pardon, as the starving beggar,
Even because he starves, can only speak
The bare word 'bread;' could I have found a way
To show him what is here, and all my need,
I know he must have pitied.
   Sey.   Is it then
So dark within thy heart? For me, I am glad

To have called thee wife before them all, and proud.
Thou'rt mine, I thine; that we have each to each
Belonged, not Heav'n itself can now undo—
And how should all be dark?

Ara.   Not all dark yet—
I have thee still. But if a bitt'rer pain
Be near, that is to make this pain seem joy,
This hour an hour stol'n out of Paradise?
Was it a dream? or was not one here now
Who said that we should part?

Sey.   One who hath power
To sunder us awhile, but not our loves.
Nay, look not so affrighted; it may be
The word was but to trap thee; it may be
They will devise a way of punishment
Other than parting.

Ara.   Ay, perchance; why not?
To imprison, or to banish—these are sounds
Harsh enough grating in the ears of most
To stand for punishment. O if 'twere so!
Might we be banished, but together still—
Denied the court—— Ah me! what joy were there!
To 'scape from spying eyes and whisp'ring tongues,
And glitt'ring glare cold as the winter moon
Mirrored in water; these to leave behind——
If you grudged not?

Sey.   How should I?

Ara.   And to live
In some fair spot of earth, where nodding boughs

Should kiss our casement, scatt'ring diamonds
Of sunshine through the shade, and the fresh morn
Come daily laden with the new sweet breath
Of wild flowers op'ning, and the air be made
Alive with music of soft-twitt'ring birds,
Who ne'er should learn to fear us. Were not this
A life foretasting Heaven?

    Sey.   Ay, so fair
That all our hope must lie in letting none
Divine how fair, for in such life no flavour
Of punishment were left.

    Ara.   Ah! now again
You set me fearing. Yea, 'tis true, for me
No punishment could be save one, and that
Hardest of all. Look, yonder comes e'en now
Our judge to bring us sentence. Hold my hand.
Doth it not seem to you that once before
In some dim past we have lived through this hour?

    Sey. So well-nigh could I deem — perchance because
What now we suffer strikes so deeply down
That 'tis become already part of us,
Familiar ere the time, and charged with tones
Of past and present blended.

    Re-enter SALISBURY, *with* SIR JAMES CROFT.

    Ara.   Pray you, sir,
What says the king? But ere you speak I know
He will be merciful.

Sal. So truly, madam,
He shows himself; and though you have to him
In disobedience and unthankfulness
Abounded, yet to you he tempers still
Justice with grace and favour.
    Ara. I knew well!
    Sal. As plain appears in this, that all your sentence
For your so grievous fault is that forthwith
You journey north to Durham, there to lodge
In the bishop's house and rev'rend custody—
You see, an easy penance. And meantime
You are commended to this gentleman,
Good Sir James Croft, who shall have charge of you,
And all that to your journey doth pertain.
    Croft. Your ladyship shall ever find in me
Your servant and the king's.
    Ara. Sirs, I am ready
To follow where you will, to come or go
As to you seems most fitting, stand or sit,
Be merry or keep silence at command,
So that the king, and you, and all that see,
Shall say my name is but another word
To signify obedience. But with me
Unto this bishop's house so far away
My husband too is sent; is this not so?
    Sal. And if 'twere so, 'twere hardly reason, madam.

He hath much offended, and his sentence is
That for his gross presumptuous revolt,
In having dared against the king's command
With one of the king's blood to join himself,
He shall be sent where he shall have full time
For pond'ring and repentance — to the Tower.
 Ara. The Tower — he to the Tower! And wherefore he?
If to be cousin to the King is fault,
The fault is mine, not his, and unto me
Should both the honour be and penalty.
Not he then to the Tower; you have mista'en.
 Sal. I have but said as I was bid to say,
And unsay can I not.
 Ara.   He to the Tower!
 Sey. Pray you, sweet wife, be patient.
 Ara.   I will speak —
This must be changed. Nay, nay, the Tower for me,
Who have offended most, and who indeed
In dreams am oft its habitant — not for him;
He must go free, or banished at the worst.
O let me see the king! this time I'll make
My prayers so strong that they shall move his heart
Perforce to pity.
 Sal.   Madam, nought avails.
The king commands, and subjects must obey.
So therefore with no further tarrying
Make your farewells, and part.
 Ara.   Part! And the Tower

Awaiting him! Awhile ago I thought
That Fate in all her armoury of ills
Had none that so could pierce me to the soul
As this of parting: but I now am taught
That even parting may be joined with worse.
Thou to the Tower! Then what for me, my love?

   Sey. I charge thee, by how much I am thy love,
Let me not see thee thus; that look of thine
Is as a murder done upon my heart.
Give me another mem'ry of thy face,
And help me to endure.

   Ara.   I will, I will,
Yea, even smile. O trust me, there is nought
For thee I could not do.

   Sey.   Remember well
While life and love are left is hope left too—
Hope that hath oft tired out the bitt'rest wrath
Of Fortune and of kings, and brought those home
In gladness who in sorrow had gone forth.
So may it be with us.

   Ara.   Ay, and so shall.
O how could I forget? What! shall I tell
How full I am of folly? in my mind
There went but even now a foolish thought
That if I lost the refuge of thine arms,
And found not one with death, I must go mad.
But thus I'll think no more; thou hast made me sure
That we shall meet again.

   Sey.   And till that time

Cherish thyself for me—rememb'ring still
Thou art my only wealth, which thou must guard,
And give me safely back.
    Ara.   I will; being thine
Makes me a thing of value to myself.
    Sal. Are you not ready?
    Sey.   Ay, my lord. I know
There's something still unsaid that I would say—
But so 'twould be had I a thousand years
To bid farewell in. Must I leave her thus,
In keeping of strange hands, with no friend near
To speak in a known voice?
    Sal.   I have sent to fetch
One of her women hither, who will give
All fitting aid and comfort. See, she comes.

Enter one of ARABELLA'S *Gentlewomen.*

    Gen. Alack! what news is this that I have heard?
O my sweet mistress! kind and gentle lady,
So gentle and so kind I hoped that harm
On you should ne'er have power.
    Sey.   Be tender with her
When I am gone, but this I know you will;
You love her well, and should. [*To* CROFT.] And you,
    good sir,
Will be a friendly gaoler; in your face
I can read pity.
    Sal.   Pray you, linger not.

Sey. Farewell, thou that art joined to me so close
No absence can prevail to make thee less
Than still a part of me, and still mine own.
    Ara. Husband, farewell. [*Exit* SEYMOUR, *with Guards.*] And now I am alone.
     [*Sinks fainting into the arms of Gentlewoman. The Curtain falls.*

END OF ACT II.

ACT III.

SCENE I.

The Garden of a Cottage near Barnet.

SALISBURY *and* CROFT *discovered.*

Sal. She knows that I await her?
Croft.   Ay, my lord,
And will come forth anon to speak with you
Here in the garden, where the air may breathe
Some strength into her weakness.
   Sal.   Fair excuse
For yet another minute of delay.
   Croft. Nay, she hath been more ailing than you deem,
But now methinks is mended far enough
That you shall find in her both power and will
To be obedient.
   Sal.   And 'tis not too soon.
What! well-nigh three moons wasted since the time
She set forth northward—the shy buds of spring
Changed to full-bosomed flowers that spread themselves
To court the sun's hot kiss—and still no more
Than an hour's ride from London!
   Croft.   Good my lord,

  Had you beheld how desp'rate was her state
When this so sudden sickness fell on her,
You would have known that you might send her corse
To Durham, not herself.
  Sal.   Well, well, you see,
We gave full time of healing and of rest
Unto the weary flesh, which, as I judge,
The impatience of her spirit had tired out.
But now I tell you, sir, the king is bent
To endure no more delay; yea, he hath sworn
To Durham she shall go, though she but make
A mile of road a day; and this command
I now am come to lay on you and her.
  Croft. And I dare promise you shall find her nought
But patient and obedient, for if once
There was a mutinous spirit in her blood,
It seems the fever hath consumed it quite,
And left her mild and meek as a dumb thing
That, after struggling, knows it must be led.
Lo you where now she comes.

   Enter ARABELLA, *leaning on the arm of her
      Gentlewoman.*

  Sal.   Most noble lady,
Take my best homage.
  Ara.   Sir, I greet you well.
  Gen. Nay, pray you, madam, sit; I know your strength
Better than you yourself.

Ara.   Kind friend—too kind
To be to me long left. My lord, they said
It was your will to see me.
    Sal.   Madam, ay—
And tell you from the king how much he joys
To know your health so mended by the time
Of rest accorded here, which in his goodness
He hath suffered to be stretched from week to week,
Against his first design. But now he deems
That this sweet country air hath med'cined you
Enough to take your broken journey up,
Therefore commands that with no more excuse
You shall set forth to-morrow.
    Ara.   I care not;
I am ready when you will.
    Sal.   I much rejoice,
As will the king, to find your ladyship
So patient in your mood.
    Ara.   What should I be?
Impatience hath burnt out, and left behind
An ash you may call patience if you will.
I have tried all ways—besought for liberty
As for a boon, and asked it as my due
Under the law of England, which methought
Left liberty to all the innocent.
But I am placed too high for law to right,
Too low for prince to favour, so am held
Inextricably in the net of Fate,
For Fate and kings to work their will upon.

Sal. Whate'er hath taught you patience, I am glad
To see the lesson learned, and will take back
To London and the king a fair report
Of you and your obedience.
　Ara.　　　　　　　　London, ay?
In London is the Tower. O tell me, sir,
How doth it fare with him? my husband—say.
　Sal. He is well, madam. Be not so disturbed.
　Ara. But in the Tower—still in the Tower?
　Sal.　　　　　　　　　　　Most sure:
Still in the Tower. I will not longer stay,
Since thus my presence moves you. Sir James Croft,
I charge you see all set in readiness
Against your morrow's journey.
　Croft.　　　　　　　　I will go
E'en now, my lord, and order each thing so
That nought shall fail. Dear madam, pardon me;
No choice is mine.
　Sal.　　　　Come then; you have much to do.
Thus humbly I salute your ladyship.
　　　　　　　　　　　　[*Exit, with* CROFT.
　Gen. Beseech you droop not thus.
　Ara.　　　　　　　　　What have I done
That you must chide? I weep not, neither sigh;
Then wherefore trouble me?
　Gen.　　　　　　　　'Twere better weep
Than sit so stony. Will you not look up
And take some joy in this sweet summer day
That smiles so fair about you?

Ara.   O I know
That the sun shines and that the flowers are out,
And butterflies on wing and birds in song,
And the air gay with flutter of green leaves,
Yea, ev'rywhere young summer triumphing
With ensigns full unfurled.   But what are these
More unto me than as the lifeless corse
Of what was beauteous once, if he sees not,
He whose partaking presence was the soul
Of all I e'er deemed fair?   And he, they say,
Still makes his darksome lodging in the Tower.
   Gen.   Think not of that.
   Ara.   What shall I think of else?
He in the Tower, walled up as in a grave,
And I to journey on beneath blue skies
Further and further from him day by day,
Grudging each step of way, yet journeying still,
Till I shall deem the space that now seems far
Was heav'nly nearness.   O might I have died
Here where I lay so sick, and where perchance
They might have let him come when I was dead
To see me laid in earth!
   Gen.   Nay, who shall say?
All may not be so desp'rate as you judge.
Be of good heart.   You have friends who love you well,
And peradventure labouring even now
 To do you service.
   Ara.   Friends I have, 'tis true,
But weaker and of less account the more

That they are friends of mine.
    Gen.   Yet doth great love
Oft render weakness strong. More would I say
If I feared not to make you hope too much.
    Ara. How mean you? hope! [*Music heard.*] Hark
        there! what music's that?
    Gen. What should it be? O I remember now.
The daughter of the farmer in the vale
Was to be wed this morn; this is the way
That they must pass to church, but sure I think
They might have had more rev'rence for this house
Than wake its quietness thus noisily.
    Ara. What! would you have me be a cloud to
        make
The joys of others dark, being dark myself?
May Heav'n forbid.

Music. Enter in procession Rustic Youths and Maidens, then a Bride with her Father and Mother, other Youths and Maidens following. As they pass along by the garden-fence, they perceive ARABELLA, *and uncover; the music stops suddenly.*

                        Friends, wherefore have you let
This silence fall upon you? See you then
Aught here that you need fear?
    Father. [*Aside to the others.*] 'Tis the great lady
From London—she herself. [*Aloud.*] An't please your
        grace,   ●
We had not thought to pass you by so close,

Or we had held our peace—for well we know
That we are but mean folk.
Ara. And therefore dread
The presence of my mightiness? but 'faith
I would not do you hurt e'en if I could.
Is't you that are the father of the bride?
Father. If so it please you, lady—but indeed
Offence there was none meant.
Ara. You have cause to boast,
If I may judge of the face she holds so low,
Of a right fair daughter. Hither, pretty maid,
Hither to me. Undo the gate, good friend,
And make her come more near.
Father. Go, my girl, go;
Great folk must have their will.
[*He opens the gate, and the Bride advances timidly.*
Ara. What! still thy face
Bent down by weight of blushes! It would seem
Thou art ashamed of how much thou art glad.
Nay, never shame of being glad, but thank
Heaven that makes thee so. Thou lov'st him well
Who waits for thee to-day? for if thou dost,
Glad thou must be, I know.
Father. See, she would die
Ere answer yea—a peevish shame-faced thing.
Now, lady, who would think that she who holds
Her mouth so tight pursed up hath faced me out,
Me and her mother too, these twelve months past,
That she would have but him, none else but him?

Ara. Was't so?

Father. Ay, was it; we had thought to find
A better for her.

Bride. Better is there none.

Father. You hear, you hear? Nay, if you'd know
  her mind,
You need but rail at him.

Ara. And for nought else
Than that she loved, and that her love was strong,
She hath prevailed at last?

Father. Why, who could bear
To see a piece of one's own flesh and blood
Pine to her grave for love, when he she loves
Is a good youth and honest? Let her be
As foolish as she will, 'tis still our child
Whom we are bound to care for.

Ara. This it is
To have a father and a mother left
To tend the life they gave—mine both were ta'en
Ere I could say I had or I had not.
But see, with idle curious questioning
I keep thee from thy waiting happiness;
I will not more. Go, child, and with thee take
This purse of gold, to pay thee for the minutes
I have made thee lose of joy.

Bride. O lady, lady,
What have I done for this?

Ara. No need for thanks;
Gold will not make thee happier than thou art—

Thou, on thy way to wed the man thou lovest,
With father, mother, kindred, smiling friends,
All standing by to bless. Give me thy hand
To say farewell. Lo! it is warm, and warms
My cold one with its heat; but of the gladness
That is within thee, and almost as near
As is this hand I hold——So now go forth,
And leave me here behind.
   Bride.   Madam——
   Ara.   Farewell;
Not a word more. Ho! let the music sound,
And all be joyful as it was before,
Made not one whit less joyful by my means.
Come—music—I command; if such as I
May give command for aught. Now go your ways,
With my good wishes following; it may be
For you they will have power.
  [*Music. The Bride and her Father make profound
     obeisances, and exeunt with the procession.*
                             I oft have heard
How the bright day with golden outstretched wings
Doth warm and cherish other lands while ours
Lies dark and cold and naked to the night—
And now I understand.
              [*The sound of a whistle is heard.*
   Gen.   O hear you that?
Lady, look up; who knows what cheerful news
May be at hand? [*The sound is repeated.*] What! there
    again! yea, sure

It must be he.
   Ara.   What mean you?
   Gen. [*Going to the side of the stage and beckoning.*
                       And he 'tis—
Come; all is safe. [*To* ARABELLA.] Madam, you know
    I said
You had friends who worked for you, and here is one—
Your trusty servant Crompton.
   Ara.   He indeed?
   Gen.   He sent me secret word that he would watch
His time to come, but this from you I hid
Lest aught should hinder.
                Enter CROMPTON.
   Ara.   O my oldest friend!
   Cromp.   My own dear lady! What! so sorrow-
    changed?
   Ara.   Not changed to you. So are you come to
    bid
Farewell before I part? for part they say
I must to-morrow—to that dreary north,
Where all things will be strange, and banishment
Begin in earnest.
   Cromp.   So in truth you must,
If nothing come between. [*To Gentlewoman.*] You have
    not yet
Told her of aught?
   Gen.   I feared to let her know
Till all were ripe, lest of too high a hope
The ruin should o'erwhelm her.

Ara.   Hope! again
That word to me! O tell me! tell me quick!
The king hath turned to mercy? What! not thus?

Cromp. Not thus indeed. But, lady, there are those
Have sworn you shall be free in his despite.

Ara. In his despite! O who are they who rate
The strength of kings so lightly?

Cromp.   One of them,
Foremost in power to aid, is your good aunt,
My Lady Shrewsbury, who on this emprise
Is bent so strongly that she sends you here
Half of her fortune turned to gold and jewels,
    [*Showing a packet which he draws from his bosom.*
To help you to deliv'rance.

Ara.   Doth she so?
O kindest kinswoman! But she knows not
How harder far achievement is than hope.

Cromp. Yet not, maybe, so hard as you account.
For here stand we, your servants, with our lives
Ready to attest our faith; and by a chance
Most helpful to our purpose it falls out
The watch about you set, that at the first
You found so close and strict and full of eyes,
Is day by day grown slacker, lulled to sleep
By the sickness which these long weeks past hath
    seemed
Your sternest gaoler, but which thus perchance
May prove to have been your friend, making those
    sluggish

Who were so wakeful once.

Gen. And in the hour
Wherein we speak they most are off their guard,
Being busied with the careful ordering
Of your new journey northward; on this task
Is your keeper now gone forth, and, as I hope,
When he returns will find his pains made vain.

Ara. What means this all? That I am to be free!
Free! and my husband not!

Cromp. Your husband too—
My life upon't—he too—and both to 'scape
Where you shall meet, and dwell with none to part.

Ara. Free!—he and I together!

Cromp. Even so—
And I now come the bearer of a message
From him to you.

Ara. From him to me!

Cromp. 'Tis this—
That he, and friends of his, have for his flight
Out of the stony keeping of the Tower
Set all in order, and he looks to-night
To be out of bondage.

Ara. He! this very night!

Cromp. Ay, out of bondage, and awaiting you
In a certain inn upon the river shore
Which with my guidance you shall find; hard by
A bark lies ready hired, whose spreading sails
Shall bear you both to France and liberty
And life-long joy, so but you have the strength

To keep this tryst he gives.
 Ara.   O never doubt;
Lead me, lead quick—I am ready.
 Cromp.   I entreat,
Keep you more calm, lest prodigal you spend
On mere expectancy the little store
Of bodily force which sickness spares you still,
And which you now must use.
 Ara.   Fear not for that;
My sickness was the sickness named despair;
Now am I well, and being well am strong.
See here how firm I stand, how firm I walk.
What! am I not of England's royal blood?
At least I have been told so oft enough—
That is, of blood which never yet ran cold
In a great task or peril; nor shall now,
If well I know myself.
 Cromp.   O this is good!
Then, dearest lady, with what speed you may,
Prepare you to come forth; a brief way hence
Our horses stay, with fretting hoofs that long
To trample distance down, and which, more chafed
By waiting, shall to London and the Thames
Full quickly bear us; for with you shall go
We twain, to share your journey and to cheer
With all due aid and service.
 Ara.   Surely none
Had e'er such friends as I. But O make haste—
Which way, which way?

Cromp. Nay, pardon, madam, first
'Tis needful with some change of outward form
To hide your proper semblance, so to pass
Disguised through all the perils that await.
Therefore, I pray you, do not scorn to don
The attire that in this wallet you will find—
A page's garb—unseemly much, I know,
But e'en for that the likeliest to our end.

Ara. Must it be so? But I'll grudge not to do
Aught that shall bring me nearer unto him.
[*To Gentlewoman.*] Beseech you come, sweet wench, and help to make
As much a man of me in outer show
As I would be in soul. O you shall see
A gallant youth, I warrant you—a youth
That shall defy the world.

Gen. So please you, madam,
Go to your chamber; I will follow straight.
[*To* CROMPTON.] Good master, come this way; I'll pour you out
A cup of wine shall brace your heart for aught
That lies before.

Cromp. 'Faith, I will not deny.
[*Exeunt into the house.*

Music. Re-enter the wedding procession, returning from church, the Bride led by her Bridegroom.

Bride. Alack! she is gone. And I who longed so much

That you should see her!
Father.　　　　　　Nay, now, as I think,
Thy longing rather was that she should see
How stout a lad thou hadst brought back from church.
　Bride.　Father! Such foolishness! But is't not
　　　pity
She should be gone? for though so high and great
I have heard her called, she looked so kind withal
That fear her could I not.
　Father.　　　　　　How would it be
Were we to sound beneath her window here
A merry stave or twain? she seemed to have
Good liking for our music.
　Bride.　　　　　　And perchance
'Twill bring her forth. Let it be so, I pray.
　　The Youths and Maidens of the procession advance
　　　　　　towards the house, and sing.

SONG.

O bright is the spring-time when meadows are green,
　And glossy buds bursting and breaking,
And blue skies lie laughing the light clouds between
　At the world from long slumber up-waking.

But of all the year round there's no season for me
Like the season of love, whate'er season it be.

O gay is the summer when flowers are unrolled,
　And trees in green bravery flaunting,

And cornfields all dimpling and rippling with gold,
  As though earth of her riches were vaunting.

But of all the year round there's no season for me
Like the season of love, whate'er season it be.

O fair is the autumn when reaping is done,
  And the forest is redd'ning and yellowing,
And in mild misty beams of the dreamy-faced sun
  The loose-dangling apples are mellowing.

But of all the year round there's no season for me
Like the season of love, whate'er season it be.

O blithe is the winter when lights are aglow,
  And fire-faggots crackling and leaping,
And folk within doors made more cheery to know
  How the wind the white snow-drifts is heaping.

But of all the year round there's no season for me
Like the season of love, whate'er season it be.

Re-enter CROMPTON, *from the house.*

Cromp.   Kind friends, for your sweet music and good will
The Lady Arabella sends you thanks;
But, being from long sickness newly risen,
She is tired, and fain would rest.
   Father.   And sir, be sure,
Full loth we were to do her aught but good.

SCENE I.] *ARABELLA STUART.* 57

Come, boys and girls, make haste; while here you
    stay
No quietness can be.
    Cromp.   Such sense she hath
Of this your friendship shown, that as her friends
She entreats you in your prayers to think of her,
And ask of Heav'n that it may send her ease.
    Bride. O this we will, doubt not—the kindest lady
That ever yet I looked on!
    Father.   So say I,
Now all get hence, as softly as you may.
[*The procession forms again, and departs. When all have
    disappeared,* CROMPTON *advances to the house.*
    Cromp. Madam, here are none left; you may come
    forth.

Re-enter from the house ARABELLA, *in boy's clothes, and
    the Gentlewoman, cloaked and veiled.*

O you are pale—too pale.
    Ara.   Indeed it seems
This strange o'er bold apparel doth but serve
To cow with contrast my too womanish heart,
So many crowding images of peril,
Unseen before, rise up on ev'ry side,
Each frighting me with threat of separate ill.
You bore in mind to ask for me the prayers
Of those kind simple folk?
    Cromp.   I asked them, madam,
And be assured they are yours. But O is this

The valiancy you promised? Think what 'tis
This enterprise, to happy ending brought,
Shall have achieved for you, and for another
More dear to you than you.

Ara. 'Tis too much thinking
Of that, which makes me weak, as the gamester's hand
Shakes at the last great throw. But you shall find
I'll keep my promise yet. I will be brave,
As in this garb I should be—yea, will play
My part so well that I shall trick perchance
Not only men that look, but Fortune's self
To take me for another than I am,
And show me favour. Well, are you not ready?
Where do those horses wait?

Cromp. This way, good madam,
So you be pleased to come.

Ara. [*To Gentlewoman.*] Give me your arm.
Nay, I forgot, 'tis I should lead forth you—
The hardy squire be guide to the feeble dame.
Lo, that fits better. O I'll grow in time
A courteous cavalier.

Gen. Alack! you shake
As a snowdrop in the wind.

Ara. And if I shake
'Tis with impatience only, trust me well.
Lead on, lead on—and Heaven's pity wait
On one whose need of pity is so great.

[*The Curtain falls.*

END OF ACT III.

ACT IV.

SCENE I.

The Deck of a Ship.

Sailors discovered hoisting a Sail. ARABELLA (*attired as at the end of Act III.*), *with* CROMPTON *and Gentlewoman, sitting a little apart.*

Sailors. [*Singing.*]   *Each man for all,*
   And all together—
    Pull, mates, pull—
   And fair shall fall
   In foulest weather.
    Pull, mates, pull.

1*st Sail.*   So, that sits bravely now; 'twill do, 'twill do.
Come, boys; there's more work aft.
 Ara.   Nay, speak I will.
 [*Detaining one of the Sailors, while his comrades withdraw.*
Pray you, a word. You kept strict watch all night,
As you were bid, on the river craft we passed,
And on the banks, and saw no signal given—

No signal from a friend, who stood and looked,
Breasting the brackish wind with outstretched arms
That pleaded for our help, while we sailed on
And left him there to wonder?

Sail.   Good faith, no;
Though we watched well—as truly we would do
Ev'rything well that we were bid to do
By a so bounteous-hearted, bounteous-handed
Young master as your honour.

Ara.   And we now
Are far upon our way—ay, quite have left
The English earth, and all it yet may hold
Of known and dear, behind?

Sail.   Why, as I take it,
We now stand half across, and with fair wind
Should sleep this night at Calais, but the breeze
Being so slack and idle as you see,
What time our captain looks to come to port
I know not, nor perchance he more than I.

    Ara. Here, friend, [*giving him money*] and when
        you see your captain next
Beseech you send him hither.

    Sail.   Sir, I will;
And were more glad to serve you for your gifts
Than others for their hire.   [*Exit.*

    Ara.   So far already
From England and from him, with this drear waste
Of glitt'ring blue between! O he knew not,
Nor knew I yesterday, he had a wife

So false and cruel, her own good to seek
He being left behind. I should have cleaved
To the trysting-place he gave till in the earth
I had ta'en root, ere let myself be drawn
To part without him.
 Cromp.   Nay, but, madam, think;
When at the trysting-place you found him not,
And waited long in vain, 'twas plain to sense
The meeting that you there had hoped was missed,
And to be sought elsewhere, for had you stayed
To be by following foes tracked out and ta'en,
You must have giv'n it up for evermore.
 Gen. 'Tis like enough, dear lady, you shall find
Whom then your eyes desired and could not see,
In France already waiting, and the first
To give you welcome.
 Ara.   Ay, so now you say
To lead me on, as yesterday you said,
To lead me on, he lay in wait for us
In the river further down; but 'twas not so—
I watched all night for sign as well as they,
And there came none; thus was I by false friends
Tricked to forsake him. O forgive, forgive;
Nor think me too unthankful for your love;
I know how great it is, but yet I fear
More great for me than him.
 Cromp.   In serving you
'Tis shown to both alike. How were't for him
If, being 'scaped himself, the tidings came

That, doubting of his fortune with no cause,
You had cast away your own, and left him lost
In a dark loveless void called liberty,
As in a spacious house of stately build,
But bare and empty-echoing? And so well
His scheme of flight was laid that scarce I think
Achievement can have failed, albeit it seems
Some chance hath hindered him from giving you
The meeting that he promised.

Ara. In good sooth
You say, and not from pity, that 'tis like
He now is not a pris'ner?

Cromp. In good sooth,
And that the greatest foe his hopes have had
Hath been yourself, by the long tarrying
You made to await him, and his truest friends
We who at last constrained you to depart.

Ara. O then I will be patient.

Cromp. Madam, look,
Here comes the captain; pray you, now, remember
More what you seem to be than what you are.

Ara. Speak you for me.

Cromp. I will, but, faith, scarce know
What you would have me say.

Ara. And all I know
Is that I pine for news he cannot give.

Enter CAPTAIN.

Cromp. Good-morrow, sir. My master, and his
    sister,
Have sent to ask you how our journey fares,
And when 'tis like to end.
    Capt.   Why, as for that,
'Twould have been nearer ended than it is
Had they not made me hither and thither tack,
And tire the wind with waiting for their friend,
Until, from being fresh and full of work,
It dropped asleep as now—and the sea too,
Which is indeed to the upper elements
The clerk who says amen, and fain must fit
His holiday with theirs.
    Ara.   Then peradventure
Before our course is done we yet may light
On him we look for, like ourselves becalmed—
Forget not well to watch.
    Capt.   Ay, ay, fear not;
I would I were your friend, to have a friend
Who took such thought for me as you for him,
And waked all night to fret and chafe and long,
As a maiden for her sweetheart.
    Cromp.   You must see,
My master having with his friend agreed
To ride o'er France in company, the sport
They looked for in the journey much is marred
By this untoward beginning.

Capt.   O I see
They are a pair of friends who ill can part.
But what of that, young sir? we who are men,
And strong and lusty and stout, as you and I,
Big-fisted, brawny-fleshed, we must hold up
Our hearts in spite of crosses, not set women
Pattern of womanishness, as, with your leave,
You set your sister here, for by my troth
You are more pale than she.
   Ara.   Perchance because
The air is something cold.
   Capt.   Cold! warm you then
With a wrestling-bout, as thus, if you scorn not
To play with me a match. Come, my young squire,
Now put forth all your mettle. Come, stand to 't.
   Cromp. Pray you, sir, cease; my master's not in mood
For idle sport.
   Capt.   Nor I in mood to try
My strength against a woman's, think it not.
What! touched I there the quick? And could you
    deem
That I could deem so dainty-white a hand,
Finished by Nature with such delicate work
Of blue-veined tracery, had at the wrist
Its base degenerate ending in a man?
No, I trow not; yet is your hand a man's,
Or will be soon, when it is giv'n in gift
To the friend you long for so.
   Ara.   Sir, sir——

Capt.   How now !
Pant not so hard; you'll fare no worse for me.
I did but speak to show you I can take
My soundings in deep water, and spy well
The master is a mistress, and those twain,
The lady-sister and the serving-man,
Your servants both alike, in like degree
Of distance standing—and the friend you seek
The other half still wanting to the pair.
Nay, nay, now, why so frighted? on my life,
I'm well inclined to lovers, and ere this
Have lent my sails to help them out of pain,
That is, the one to the other.
　　Cromp.   She hath borne
So much of late that ev'ry breath that blows
Wakes mem'ry of past ill and fear of new.
But see, she trusts you now, and smiles again.
　　Capt. Why, that is well—I warrant her all things
Will fall as she would have them; folk in love,
I oft have seen, come ever safe to port;
For Cupid whom they serve is as a wag
Who puffs his cheeks and sputters wind and rain,
But e'en by reason of his waggishness
Will do no deadly harm. I have helped those
Harder to help than lovers.
　　Ara.   So? And who?
　　Capt. Those whom the state hath looked askance
　　　upon.
There is the pinch of pinches, then the time

To keep the hand on the helm—no blithesome breeze
To brag and bounce and bluster in your teeth,
Only a little cloud out of the sea
That rises, ever dark'ning. But for you,
Be of good cheer; you lovers are too trifling
For Fortune long to keep her spite against.

Enter a Sailor.

Well, well! what would you have?
   Sail.   Look, sir, a ship—
A ship to windward, pressing on our track,
With signals up to bid us stay our course.
   Ara. O then 'tis he at last!
   Capt.   Not so, not so;
You see, 'tis a king's ship; and sure enough
Would speak with us, but why 'tis hard to know.
   Ara. A king's ship, say you?
   Capt.   Ay, but where's the harm?
We carry nought forbid; when they have found
Their error out, they will not hinder long.
Bring to, and wait.
   Ara.   No, no! On—onward still!
[*To* CROMPTON.] O tell! I have no breath.
   Cromp.   By all the love
That e'er you bore to sister or to wife,
Mother, or tender daughter, hold you now
Your course; by us you shall be tenfold fee'd,
And thousandfold by Heaven.

Capt.   Stands it thus?
'Tis worse than I had deemed. Well, all I can
To serve you will I do, but if my pains
Will aught avail I know not; they that follow
I fear are better trimmed than we to catch
What little wind there stirs. And then king's ships
Have with them oft a certain loud-voiced way
That makes them heard from far, and, heard, obeyed.
                               [*A shot is heard.*
So, hark you there. Not near enough as yet
To do us hurt, but like to be full soon.
    Ara. O onward still! Save! save!
    Capt.   Ay, if I can.
Poor wench, with all my soul I pity thee.
What ho! boys, give not in. Keep up your hearts,
And ev'ry sail full stretched.
        [*A volley of firing is heard. More Sailors appear.*
    1*st Sail.*   How! shall we sink
Only to pleasure you? Bring to! strike flag!
    Other Sailors. Ay, ay, well said! strike flag!
    Capt   Why then, strike flag,
And have your way—for, lady, on my word,
There's no way else; to stand another round
Were but to play at ninepins with our lives.
    Ara. I was to blame, but I forgot that life
Could still be dear to any. I am glad
The pain of hope is o'er—for well I knew
What was to be the end, and now 'tis come,
And I have nought to do but rest and wait,

And cease from strife, being conquered.

[*Seats herself.*

Capt. Lo you there !
Descrying that we yield, they send a boat
Wherewith to reach us sooner, which e'en now
Glides from the tall ship's shadow—ay, the oars
Will make short work with distance—and, you see,
Brimful of arméd men.

Cromp. Alas! alas!
This stroke hath crushed her quite.

Gen. Madam, take heart.

Ara. You pity me too much; there is no need;
To me 'tis all as though I but looked on,
And saw this evil on another fall—
Save that methinks another in this plight
Would move me to more feeling.

Capt. Yea, I said
Their oars would bring them fast. Be ready, boys,
To heave them down a rope—'faith, would we dared
Haul them aboard by the necks.

Gen. What! do they come?
O lady, lady, hide; it yet may be
They shall not find you.

Ara Have you ever heard
Of a hiding-place so dark and still and safe
That Fate found not the prey she once had marked?
And me she long hath marked, and now the time
To strike me down is come.

Capt. So there, they touch;

Ay, for the weight they carry they climb well.
Yet well or ill, should not the lubberly brood
Be boarding us, were we but armed as they.
[*Turning to* ARABELLA.] How goes it now? Nay, be
    not so dismayed.
    Gen. She will not hide. But O betray her not.
    Capt. Betray! not I; as a fish I will be dumb—
Albeit, I fear, of no more use to help.
See, see, they come.
    Gen. [*To* CROMPTON.] Stand you in front with me,
And hide her while we may.

        Enter an Officer, with Guards.

    Off. Which is the captain here?
    Capt.   An't please you, sir,
Captain am I. [*Aside.*] Would I were master too!
    Off. Then from this warrant will you see I have
    power
To make search for, and seize wherever found,
The person of the king's near kinswoman,
The most illustrious Lady Arabella,
Who, having first offended by transgression
Against his high command, hath now dared break
From his just durance. We have cause to deem
She is here with you embarked.
    Capt.   By Heav'n above,
Then know you more than I; so great a dame
Is far too great for passenger of mine.
    Ara. [*Rising and coming forward.*] Enough, enough;

                          I thank you, but here let
All bootless torment end.   Sir, I am she,
The Lady Arabella that you seek,
Who, were I what by attire I ape to be,
Had sold to-day my liberty as dear
As English prince did ever.   But I came
Into the world for sorrow, and, that sorrow
Should have on me full power, ordained a woman ;
So therefore do I yield.
     Off.   And on my part,
Madam, I arrest you, and declare you here
The pris'ner of the king.
     Ara.   Do what you will ;
To me 'tis now all one.
     Off.   Ere more be said,
Tell me—What of the other whom we seek,
Your husband, and partaker of your fault
In disobedience and in flight alike ?
Answer and tell forthwith.
     Ara.   You ! is it you
Ask news from me ?   'Scaped then and free !   Is't
     true
You know not of him ?
     Off.   Nought but that last night
He broke from out the keeping of the Tower,
And fled we know not whither ; 'tis for you
To say the rest.
     Ara.   And I can say but this,
That you have made me glad—yea—O how glad !

More glad a thousandfold than e'er you thought
To make me sorry. Pardon me, sweet Heaven,
I see that still you live, and still keep watch
Even for such as I.

    Off.   If true it be
The other pris'ner whom we seek hath 'scaped,
I am well pleased it makes you so content,
Since I have now in charge to see you borne
Unto the Tower, that Tower whence he is fled.
But which for you may prove a stricter ward
Than it hath been for him. I pray you, madam,
Be patient of the escort of these guards,
Who now must lead you thither.
                      [Guards surround ARABELLA.

    Ara.   What of that?
Welcome the Tower, welcome all things for me
Mine is the triumph still, for he is free.
                        [The Curtain falls.

END OF ACT IV.

ACT V.

SCENE I.

A Room in the Tower.

ARABELLA *discovered with a Woman-Attendant. The latter is at work;* ARABELLA *sits gazing before her, with her work lying in her lap.*

Ara. So weary—O so weary! These long days
Wherein time hath no motion, and yet brings
To me no rest—so many and so long!
[*To Attendant.*] Since when, by the world's count,
    have I lived here?
Att. Madam, four years.
Ara.   Nay, nay, you mock me now;
'Tis years agone since first you said four years.
Att. By fullest reck'ning four years, and three
    moons.
Ara. No more than that! I do remember well
In my other life to have heard them say the Tower
Was grim and dull, and now I find it true.
But he—he hath a better dwelling-place;

In France the sun shines warm, and skies are blue,
And the air brisk and blithesome, and all things
Dancing with very brightness—is't not so?
    Att. So have I heard, good madam.
    Ara.   Ay, but still
He thinks of me; how pleasantly soe'er
The broad blue freedom of the horizon smiles,
He thinks of me; I feel him with me oft.
I tell you, wench, he loves me; will you doubt?
But you perchance ne'er knew him.
    Att.   Ne'er in sooth.
    Ara. 'Tis pity. Were you one of my old servants,
Who knew him well, we had held much discourse.
But they and ev'ry face that once looked kind
Are ta'en away, and I left quite alone.
    Att. Dear lady, say not so, for here am I,
Albeit no more than a rough gaoler's wife,
Will serve you all I can.
    Ara.   O pardon me;
'Tis true that you are kind, and true besides
I give you much to bear with and to do,
So ailing as I am, and in my brain
Sometimes, I fear—though I know not if e'er
You have noted it—a little wandering.
Have you not thought it too?
    Att.   Nay, 'tis not wise
To give such fancies harbour.
    Ara.   Hark! what noise?
Who comes? O who?

Enter a Warder.

Att. 'Tis but my husband, madam.
Ara. Ay, only he? And by his face I see
There is no mercy yet. O when will't come,
The mercy that I ask? I have asked so oft—
And 'tis not much to ask; a little mercy
In God's name, that is all.
War. So please you, madam,
The Lady Shrewsbury, being moved to hear
How your health droops of late, hath sued for leave
To see you for a space, and sends me now
To warn you that she comes.
Ara. She! who is she?
War. The Lady Shrewsbury.
Ara. Shrewsbury, said you?
Ay, ay, 'tis so—my aunt—my good kind aunt—
O what of her?
War. She comes to see you, madam,
Having thereto got leave.
Ara. Let it not be;
To find me here would vex her overmuch,
Yea, make her chide perchance. Tell her to wait
Till I be better lodged; 'twill not be long.
War. Why, madam, you forget; she is herself
Used to no better place; here in the Tower
She hath dwelt as long as you.
Ara. And for what cause?

O I know now—for this; [*looking down at herself*]
    this is a cause
Hath made full many suffer, and in prison
Pine the long hours away. Ah! how I pity
Them and all pris'ners else! But I am glad
He is not of them.

    Enter LADY SHREWSBURY, *conducted by another Warder, who remains present.*

  Lady Sh.   Well, poor cousin, well!
And so we meet at last—but, as I think,
Too late for you to know me.
  Ara.   Nay, not so;
I know you, and I love you—[*kissing her*] for I see
You are my good aunt still, and my kind friend,
Though sometimes you are stern—but now with me
You will be stern no more?
  Lady Sh.   I heard you ailed—
But I knew not how much.
  Ara.   'Tis not my fault;
I've tried to be made well, and tried to live—
O tried how hard to live! for many a time
Have I been tempted much, but would not yield,
Knowing that to be cause of one's own death
Is an unchristian thing, that might perchance
Part me from him for ever.
  Lady Sh.   Yet may grief
Be murderous as hands; so this poor face
Doth all too clearly witness.

Ara.   Seem I then
So changed from what I was—changed it may be
Beyond his knowledge? This is what I feared—
That he, who lives in the sunshine and the air,
Will come with fresh cheeks back, and find mine sunk,
And faded, and unworthy of his kiss.
You are not changed—O teach me how to do
That at our meeting he shall see me still
The wife he left—for meet I know we shall
One day—he said it.
   Lady Sh.   You would be as I?
Then think not of your friends, but of your foes,
Rejoicing while you languish; and resolve
To cheat them of their triumph.
   Ara.   Is't indeed
The way you take?
   Lady Sh.   Ay, and a way to man
The poorest heart with strength. Why, child, ere now
I might be free would I have stooped to sue
Our Scotch schoolmaster's pardon; but I bear
A loftier soul within me, that, like iron,
Hardens by being beat on. Be as I,
Make front against your foes, and live and thrive.
   Ara. This were to live by hate, but love it is
I need to make me live—love that I pine for
As hunger doth for food and thirst for drink,
And perish being shut from.
   Lady Sh.   'Tis e'en thus;
The strength that for defiance you should keep

You waste in idle sorrow.
Ara.   Idle—yea—
Too idle—I forgot. Give me my work;
Now will I make good speed. There's much depends
Upon this work of mine—more than you think.
    Lady Sh. So, niece? and what?
    Ara.   Look, 'tis a tapestry
I broider for the king—pray you tell not.
I sent it once before, but for his use
'Twas too sad-coloured, and he sent it back.
    Lady Sh. Ay, did he thus?
    Ara.   'Tis true, and therefore now
I work it o'er again with gayer threads,
Till it be fit for a king's eye, and bright
As a fair summer morning in the fields;
So must it surely please him, and if pleased
He'll be my friend again, and all that's past
Will seem an ugly dream. You see, you see
What need I have for diligence.
    Lady Sh. [*To 1st Warder.*]   Is't oft
So dark with her as now?
    1st War.   E'en as to-day
You find her, hath she been full long, unchanged,
Saving that her physician makes report
Her strength of late wanes faster.
    Lady Sh.   And he gives
No hope of better?
    1st War.   Madam, none, but says
She cannot long endure, scorched as she is

By a fierce fever always, that drinks up
From hour to hour her life-blood.
　　Att.　　　　　　　　　　Yet nathless
Despair he cannot quite, since he has asked
Of the lieutenant leave to bring to-day
A doctor friend he hath, of special skill,
He thinks, to soothe brain-sickness such as hers;
Pray Heav'n that so it prove! This very hour
He did appoint to come, and bring with him
Her new physician.
　　Lady Sh.　　　　And a wise physician
He who can do her good must surely be.
　　2nd War.　　[*Advancing to* LADY SHREWSBURY.
　　Madam, the minutes here accorded you
Are fully measured out; so must I pray
That unto your apartment you be pleased
To make return forthwith.
　　Lady Sh.　　　　　　　Ha! man!—Be't so;
We pris'ners may not choose. Niece, fare you well;
I must not longer stay.
　　Ara. [*Still at her work.*] Farewell, farewell;
I'd rise to do you honour, but you see
The straits I'm in for time. I must work hard.
　　Lady Sh. God pity you, poor child! Nor can I think
That He will let the king, and the king's son,
And grandson, sit the safer on their throne,
Or die the happier in their beds, because
Thou art brought down to this.　　[*Exit, with* 2*nd*
　　　　Warder. The 1*st Warder also withdraws.*

SCENE I.]   *ARABELLA STUART.*   79

Ara.   How meant she that?
For who hath ever lived that could be made
Happy because another is not so?—
And I am not; although I seem to be,
I am not really.   Nay, with these thoughts
Mine eyes grow dim, and cannot see to work;
Give me my lute; I'll sing, and will not weep;
Much weeping hurts the eyes, as I have found,
And I have need of mine.   What joyous theme
Shall I find out to sing of?   I have heard
Nought is so pleasant in the world as love.
             [*Takes up a lute, and tries to sing.*
        Love, smiling love,
        What so happy and fair,
           Below or above,
        In the earth or the air?
[*Breaks into bitter weeping.*]   I cannot help—indeed I
    cannot help.
   Att.   Alas! poor lady!   Come into your chamber,
And rest you on your bed; a little sleep
Were your best med'cine.
   Ara.   Yea, if I could sleep
'Twere well; in sleep there is forgetting.   Come;
I'll do whate'er you bid me; you are kind.
                [*Exeunt into an inner room.*

Re-enter 1st *Warder, ushering in* SEYMOUR, *disguised in a cloak and hood, and a Physician.*

   War.   This way, good master doctor.   What! it seems

She's in her chamber; shall I call her forth?
　Phy.　Nay, nay, disturb her not; there is no haste,
And I will profit by the time we wait
To unfold unto my fellow-doctor here,
More fully than he knows them yet, the signs
Of the malady wherewith he hath to cope.
Therefore, beseech you, leave us.
　War.　　　　　　　I obey,
And will pray Heav'n your counsels may avail
For the poor lady's good.　　　　　　　[*Exit.*
　Phy.　　　　　　Sir, for God's love,
Remember now your promise, and take heed
You abandon nought of that feigned outward semblance
Wherein you hide yourself; bethink you well
That if suspicion once pierce through the rind
Of your disguise unto the man you are,
You will be wholly lost.
　Sey.　　　　　　Lost! what is't then
That you call lost?
　Phy.　　　　　　O trifle not.　You know
That if through any chink the tidings crept
You dared draw breath again in English air,
Ay, now stood here within the very walls,
Not used to being mocked, of that same Tower
You cheated once, the heavy-sounding doors
Would close on you with thunder as of doom,
To open nevermore.
　Sey.　　　　　　And if 'twere so,
Would it fare worse with me than now with her?

Phy.   You care not for yourself; but pray you show
Some little heed for me, whom you have drawn
In peril for your sake.   You'll say perchance
You bought my friendship, yet, believe me well,
Not all the gold wherewith so bounteously
You plied my poverty had moved me e'er
To meddle in a bus'ness of such risk
But that I pitied you with all my heart,
And your great hunger of beholding her.
Repay me not with ruin.
   Sey.   Have no fear;
I will be wary.   You have pitied me,
And I am thankful much.
   Phy.   I could not choose
But feel some pity of a husband's longing
To look on his wife's face, the more that soon
The time will have gone by that earthly power
Can ever show it him.
   Sey.   You are careful still
To arm me for the worst.
   Phy.   Because unarmed
It may be you would lack the strength to bear
The sight of her so changed.
   Sey.   So changed, think you,
She will not know me?
   Phy.   Sir, sir, are you mad?
Heav'n send she know you not, for what she knows
She is too distraught to have the art to hide;
So would her knowledge wreck us all.   Is this

G

The promise that you gave me?
 Sey.   Ay, indeed—
My promise—I forgot—but never doubt;
I will fulfil; although the task be hard
To look on her, and not to speak her name
And call her mine—but yet it shall be done.
 Phy. It must be done, and truly for her sake
No less than ours; for, sir, I tell you this,
The elements that make her mortal part
Do with such feebleness cohere, a breath
Of perturbation might disjoin them quite,
As wind blots out a bubble.
 Sey.   Is it so?
I will heed well.
 Phy.   And thus perchance may win
Another and another sight of her,
Nay, even so accustom her at last
To see and hear you that your voice may serve
To soothe her wearied sense, as a loved strain
Of music may, albeit where first 'twas heard
We cannot call to mind; so might you prove
Indeed her best physician. But beware.
 Sey. I will, I will.
 Phy.   And be in all things ruled
As I give sign—to speak or hold your peace,
E'en as by my observance of her mood
I shall deem safe and fitting.
 Sey.   Trust me well.
O what comes here? She? she indeed?

Phy.   Stand back.
Re-enter ARABELLA, *followed by Attendant.*
Ara.   No sleep for me—I shall be best at work.
Ha! who are these? You, sir, I know—but he—
Who should he be?
Phy.   Madam, the new physician
I have found leave to bring. Friend, is't not so?
Sey.   E'en so—your new physician.
Ara.   Speak again—
Again! I heard not clear.
Phy.   Madam, how now!
Why are you so disturbed? this is not well;
What! must I chide outright?
Ara.   'Tis that there goes
A quiv'ring through my brain, as when the lightning
Of a summer night throbs in and out, and shows,
And takes away ere we have rightly seen.
Will he not speak again?
Phy.   Nay, on my word,
If by a stranger's sight you are so moved,
I must fain send him hence.
Ara.   No need, no need!
I'll govern well myself—O you shall see.
Phy.   So then sit down, and tell me of your state.
Sir, stand aloof, I pray, till to your presence
She is grown more used. Madam, regard him not,
And give your thoughts to me, if you indeed
Would have me do you good.
Ara.   In truth I would—

And will obey you as a little child,
So you will show me how I may be well;
For, sir, I must live—must; I have in France
A husband unto whom I am under bond.
He bade me live; 'twas his command I should;
He said I was his wealth, his only wealth,
That I for him must guard. You scarce would think
That I, so weak and broken as I am,
Could be of any man the only wealth—
But so indeed he said. What sound was that?
   Phy. Nought, nought. I pray you, madam, look
      at me,
And gather up your thoughts.
   Ara.   Where was I? Yea—
His wealth—'twas thus he said—and, 'faith, sometimes
I wish he had not said; sometimes I wish
I had his leave to die, for, as you see,
To me life brings small good, and some my death
Might profit much; with one to-day I spoke
Who lives in prison for my sake, and others
There are, my poor old servants, for me punished—
And I away, their punishment would cease;
And he, he then were free to tread once more
The English earth he loves, and show himself
Of Englishmen the stateliest. Ay, sure,
I were best dead, albeit he bade me live.
   Phy. 'Tis not well, madam, on these things to
      think.
   Ara. Deem not I fear to die—in good sooth no.

Could I but die, I might be born again
In another world, where princesses are not,
And royal blood ne'er heard of; there might I,
A lowly shepherd's daughter, meet with him,
A neighbour shepherd's son, in the fresh fields
All daisy-starred, with nought 'twixt us and heaven;
There might we woo, there wed, with loving faces
Of dear friends round us, and yet each to each
More dear than all, there live our lives for love,
As to be lived they were given.
[SEYMOUR *breaks into sobs.*]   Hark! his voice—
His—tell me not—I know—his, his—'tis he!
[*Rushing towards* SEYMOUR, *who stands with his face
  buried in his hands.*
Look on me! look! What! will you shut me out?
Out of thine arms in the darkness and the cold?
Open, and let me in.
   Sey.   Ay, to thy home,
Thy home upon my heart. My wife! my love!
               [*Clasping her to his breast.*
   Phy. [*To Attendant.*] If e'er you felt one throb of
      pity stir
For her sorrows and her gentleness, let fall
No word of this.
   Att.   Betray her could I not,
Though bribed with all the world.
   Sey.   Lift up thine eyes;
I have yearned long enough; rob me not now.
O me! she swoons! Help, help, I pray you help!

[*They lay her down, her head resting on* SEYMOUR'S *knee.*
Gently, more gently.   Nay, I'll hold her still;
You shall not part us.   Wife, dost thou not hear?
'Tis I that call—thy husband—look and see—
Thy husband—see.   [*Throws off his cloak.*
                    Wife! wife!—Ah! sure I was
That word would be of power to unclose her eyes—
And O thou knowest me! thou smilest!
   Ara.   Yea,
I know that thou art found, and the cloud gone—
That darksome cloud wherein I wandered lost—
And I am I again, being joined with thee.
Have I not cause to smile?
   Sey.   O mine own love,
How have I longed for this!
   Ara.   Ay, hold me fast
In thy strong arms, those arms that plucked me forth
From the realm of darkness and of night, those arms
That brought me back unto myself and thee.
   Sey.   Doubt not, doubt not; they so shall cleave
       and grow
To their lost treasure found, that easier
'Twill be to tear them from the shoulders off
Than make them give thee up.
   Ara.   And yet methinks
Give up they must full soon.
   Sey.   How dost thou mean?
None shall divide us now; not our worst foes
Would have the heart; and these, you see, are friends,

Good friends, who, when they find that we are bent
To brook no parting, will devise a way
To help us forth together from this place—
Will you not, friends? and let us seek far hence
Beyond the seas some corner of the earth
Where she and I may live, with none made worse
Or poorer for our loves, and we ourselves
Out of all measure rich.
 Ara.   O know'st thou not?
Husband—belov'd—I am dying.
 Sey.   Dying! nay,
Thou mak'st me well-nigh smile. In faith, not dying;
I'll kiss that fear away.
 Ara.   If 'twere but fear,
Thy kiss would cure it, sure; but not e'en thou
Canst heal what death hath touched.
 Sey.   Dare not again
Speak to me thus. Is then thy love so small
That, being but newly found, thou wouldst away,
And never see me more?
 Ara.   Never! who says
That death means never? Have we not before us
Eternity to seek each other in?
And will you set upon eternity
The limit of a never? that word never
Is a word eternity's too vast to hold.
 Sey. O with that look upon thy face thou seemest
Far off from me already. Stay—come back!
Wife! pity, pity! wife!

Ara.   Lament me not;
I am happy, wondrous happy, and should be more
But for thy sorrow sounding in mine ears,
Which seems to draw me down while I would rise.
O let it cease with me, and when I am dead,
And thou wouldst weep, think I have had such hours
Of gladness in my life, though with long spaces
Of weariness between, that my full sum
Of joy hath been made up, nor would I change
With those who are deemed more favoured; and besides,
Think all this happiness that I have known
Hath come to me through thee, and loving thee,
And being by thee loved; and thinking thus
Live happy all thy days—and love me still.

   Sey.   Ay, will I, while my soul doth know herself.

   Ara.   And 'twill be well; in love is the best life;
I doubted once, but now I doubt no more—
Heav'n's choicest gift to earth, e'en as they say.
There was a song—I think to hear it yet—

                                      [*Sings faintly.*]

        Love, smiling love,
           What so happy and fair,
        Below or above,
           In the earth or the air?

True—yea, all true; here in my heart I feel
Its sunshine now—so smiling—happy and fair.

   Att.   Lady! Alas! how faint doth grow her breath!

Ah! ope your eyes, and look on us once more.
  Phy. Peace, peace; distract her not.
  Ara. [*Raising herself suddenly.*] Husband, time was
We made a tryst and missed it, but this tryst
We will not break; yonder I'll welcome thee.
Till then be happy—happy e'en as I.   [*Dies.*
  Phy. Gone.
  Sey.   Gone! Can Heaven let this be? O why?
           [*Casts himself down beside* Arabella's *body.*
                                          The Curtain falls.

THE END.

THE HEIR OF LINNE.

H

PERSONS REPRESENTED.

LIONEL, LORD OF LINNE.
LORD FITZWATER,
SIR RUFUS ROLLESTONE, } *Guests staying in Lionel's House.*
HUBERT, *Son to Lord Fitzwater,*
JOHN OF THE SCALES, *Steward to Lionel.*
TOM TOD, *an old Tenant.*

LADY FITZWATER, *Wife to Lord Fitzwater.*
GERALDINE, *their Daughter.*
AMABEL,
LETTICE, } *Sisters to Sir Rufus Rollestone.*
JOAN, *Wife to John of the Scales.*
LILIAS, *Niece to John.*

Other Guests, Servants, &c.

The Scene is laid in Lionel's House and Park.

ACT I.

'His father was a right good lord,
   His mother a lady of high degree;
But they, alas! were dead him fro,
   And he loved keeping company.'
         Old Ballad of *The Heir of Linne.*

THE HEIR OF LINNE.

ACT I.

SCENE I.

A Park. On one side, towards the back of the stage, is seen part of a large and stately house. On the other, nearer the front, is a ruined ivy-grown cottage, with over-hanging balcony approached by a worn flight of steps.

JOHN OF THE SCALES *discovered, with a bundle of bills in his hand.*

John. To vintner due nine thousand crowns, nine
    hundred—
Why not have made it ten? cheese-paring knave—
Then to silk-mercer seven thousand odd
For hanging guest-chambers; were the guests mine
I'd rather pay the hanging of them too.
Then tailor comes, and goldsmith, clock-maker,
Coach-maker, harness-maker, and a dozen
Such beggar-makers else. Ay, ay, my day
Draws on apace, the day that all my life

I've toiled and sweated for, the day that I,
E'en I, whom men call John of the Scales in mock,
Being but a weigher-out of others' goods,
Shall see myself a lord o'er that same land
Where I have been a servant—lord of Linne.
And others too shall see; that roistering crew
Of guests who fill the house and eat it up—
Working for me, not knowing—they shall see,
And doff the cap, and say, 'Well met, fair sir,
How do you, sir, to-day, and your good dame?'
They who now brush me by with no more heed
Than though I were a joint-stool in their way.
And I shall say, 'Sweet lords, sweet ladies, thanks;
I kiss your hands;' and they will say, 'We yours;'
So shall we purr together all day long,
But lick me bare they shall not; I am made
Of other stuff than that young crowing cock
Who tosses o'er his head in wantonness
His overplus of grains—that scattergood,
Sieve-pocketed, sieve-brained, who for a while
Still calls himself my master.

Enter LIONEL.

Lion. What! good John?
Back from your errand? Pardon, I knew not
You were so deep in thought.

John. [*Hiding away the bills.*] My thoughts were all
Of you, my lord, and of your business.

Lion. No need to tell me that, old faithful friend.
And you have brought the jewels?
    John.   Ay, sir, here—
                                    [*Producing a casket.*
The richest I could buy in all Carlisle.
I hope they are chosen well; with my poor best
I strove to please your lordship.
    Lion.   .That I know;
Come, let me see. [*Opening the casket.*] A necklace
    first of pearls,
Fine as though formed of Beauty's tears congealed,
And white enough to lie heaved up and down
On the whitest neck that is, and not be shamed.
This likes me well. And next—of lesser cost,
And yet not poor—a bracelet of graved gold
Bossed o'er with rubies, worthy well to make
A dainty wrist its willing prisoner;
This is good too. And then a half-score more
Of golden toys—clasps, brooches, and the like—
But each set with a gem of price that gives
To its slightness patent of nobility;
A well-judged choice indeed. [*Looking round.*] Quick,
    put them up;
They must not yet be seen.

Enter, from the house, SIR RUFUS ROLLESTONE, AMABEL, *and* LETTICE, *in archery costume, with bows and arrows.*

                            Ha! now I know

That these fair ladies think they have well-nigh
Surprised a secret, but upon my life
An honest secret 'tis, and one that soon
Their eyes shall look on, and their hands shall touch.
Well, for the contest you are full equipped?
    Amab. O yes, my lord, and burning to make proof
Of Amazonian skill.
    Lett.   Which is the way
That we must take unto the battle-field?
    Lion. On the smooth sward that lies beyond the copse
The targets are set up; your brother knows
The nearest path; he'll be your guide and guard.
And guard them well, Sir Rufus, for the shafts
Shot by their eyes may make them more assailed
Than the arrows in their hands will make them feared.
    Amab. Assailed! who should assail us, good my lord?
    Lion. A little fellow-archer, who, doubt not,
Hath marked you for his prey. You'll find, methinks,
Most of our company already met,
To whom beseech you say I'll come anon,
And play my part of umpire.
    Sir Ruf.   And till then
We'll leave you with your mystery all alone.
A mystery and a mistress are two things

SCENE I.] *THE HEIR OF LINNE.*

'Tis always better for the owner of
To be alone with. This way, sisters—come.
 Amab. Of that same archer more another time.
   [*Exeunt* SIR RUFUS, AMABEL, *and* LETTICE.
 Lion. Too liberal of wit, and tongue, and eyes,
Both these; my choice is best.
 John.   Is it for them
The jewels are, my lord?
 Lion.   What! know you not?
They are prizes for the ladies, my fair guests,
Who try their skill in this day's shooting match.
For the best score the necklace; the next best
Shall bear away the bracelet; and the rest
Find comfort in those trinkets, since shame 'twere
Any should part no richer than they came
From where I'm master.
 John.   You will keep, I see,
Your golden name of being in all the north
The lord of fullest purse and freest hand.
And for the gentlemen the prizes are——
 Lion. Horses that each shall choose at his good will
Out of my stables. O I'll not fall short
Of what fame makes me out.

Enter, from the house, LORD *and* LADY FITZWATER, HUBERT, *and* GERALDINE, *the last two in archery costume.*
       Now, in good time,

Of all my guests most honoured. Lord Fitzwater,
To you, and to your ladyship, much thanks
That you vouchsafe your presence at our sports.

Lord F. Nay, 'tis a joy, believe me well, a joy—
And, when the sun is out, not damp at all.

Lady F. And if it were, for you he would brave much.

Lion. I hope, and nothing doubt, that for your pains
You'll see your daughter's arrow wing its way
Victorious to the centre.

Geral.   O for that
I fear my courage will not serve to-day.
Some, being watched, are made thereby more bold,
But I am not of those—would that I were!
Ah! how you men, that are so brave and strong,
Must scorn a coward!

Lady F.   And to-day, poor child,
She's more a coward even than her wont—
So full of foolish flutters with no cause.
Indeed since here at Linne she hath been a guest
I oft have feared that something ails my girl,
But know not what.

Lion.   You think not 'tis the place
That suits her ill?

Lady F.   The place! nay, nay, fear not;
As for the place, it suits her as no place
Suited her yet. O she is wondrous well.
Where are the sports to be?

Lion.   Hubert, you saw
Where they had pitched the tent; pray you conduct
Your father and your mother to the seats
Of chiefest honour 'mong the lookers-on,
While you and your fair sister join yourselves
Unto the ranks of archers.
    Hub.   Yes. I hope
That none will be before me in the choice
Of the star-chested bay; there is a horse
I'm set upon.
    Lion.   Or so at least shall be—
For since you are run away with by the bay
He shall be yours, although I buy him back
Of the winner double-priced. No thanks, no thanks;
You make your father wait.
    Lord F.   Now to the tent;
In the tent we shall be better; though indeed
This is a kind of Eden you have here,
And the trees the oldest trees that e'er I saw,
And the sunshine brightest, and the wind, for wind,
Marvellous soft—in faith, a joy to feel—
Still in the tent we shall be out of it.
    Lion. Good Hubert, lead the way; I'll follow
        straight.
Fair Lady Geraldine, be very sure,
All tim'rous as you are, you shall not fail
To-day of conquest.
    Geral.   Deem you so in truth?

Yet am I tim'rous still.
> [*Exit with* LORD *and* LADY FITZWATER *and* HUBERT.

Lion. And O how bravely
Her tim'rousness doth show! Tell me, good John,
What think you of that lady?

John. There were here
Two ladies; is't the young or old you mean?

Lion. Come, come, thou foolish fellow, well thou knowest.
And hark, I have a mind that she I mean
Shall be, if so she please, Lady of Linne.
What say you of my choice?

John. [*Aside.*] She hath no dower,
And will but help her lord to spend more fast.
[*Aloud.*] I say your choice is worthy well of you,
My excellent good master.

Lion. Thanks, kind friend.
I'm glad my purpose finds you so content,
Since it is well-nigh fixed; and, sooth to tell,
She is the guest for whom the rest were asked,
And for whose pleasure, as I can, I seek
Each day new pastime, and on whose white neck
I hope to set those pearls, since with her bow
She is skilled as Dian's self. I have dreamed long
That in her eyes, when I draw near—albeit
As soon as she hath looked she looks away—
A light of welcome kindles.

John.   I should marvel
Were't otherwise, my lord, [*Aside*] since she is poor,
And he, in seeming, rich.
   Lion.   And time it is
That I should wed at last; too long already
I have tarried, waiting for I know not what;
Some bright impossible maid, some counterpart
That never was nor ever yet shall be
To dreamy longings such as sometimes come
To a youthful foolish heart—say in the pause
'Twixt day and night that a spring twilight brings,
When hawthorn blossoms rock themselves to sleep,
And no sound stirs save from the nested birds
A twitter here and there, and the faint stars
Steal forth from the paling sky, and in our souls,
All else being lulled to rest, vain yearnings wake.
But I will rather turn unto the real,
And with a thankful mind take what it gives—
A fair maid and a kind, of equal birth,
To double all I have of happiness
With sweet companionship.
   John.   And you do well,
Nor better could I wish.
   Lion.   Give me the jewels;
I must go share them out. O but first stay—
Have you not noted that when each fair guest
Shall have her prize two trinkets will be left?
   John. I bought, my lord, but what you bade me buy.
   Lion. I know, and these two more I bade you buy

For Joan, and for Lilias your niece,
That they may not be the only ones to go
Without a gift to-day. Bid them come straight;
They shall be first to choose.
John.   O my kind lord,
Such honour they are not worth—although indeed
My wife, poor soul, prays for you morn and night.
Lion. Call them, I say.
John. [*Calling towards the house.*] What! Joan,
  wife, come forth,
And make good speed; our lord would speak with
  you.
Lion. And Lilias too, I pray.

Enter JOAN.

John.   And Lilias too.
Niece! She is always last.
Lion.   She was last called.
Joan, how now! Give you good-morrow, dame.
Joan. My lord is ever kind. [*Aside.*] Should this
  be all
He hath to give to-day?
Lion.   I called you hither—
But where is Lilias?
John.   Here at last, my lord.

Enter LILIAS.

Lion. Be welcome, little maiden. You are called,
And you, good Joan, that you each may choose

From these the brooch or clasp that to your liking
Shall most commend the giver. Joan, come;
You are the oldest friend; you first shall speak.

Joan. Now see you there! Lilias, have I not said
There ne'er was lord in all the world like ours,
So liberal and so lordly in his mind,
And who in giving hath such taking ways?
Have I not said it, Lilias? are you dumb?

Lili. 'Tis true that we have found him bountiful.

Lion. Come, make your choice.

Joan.   'Tis sore against
    my will;
But for your sake, my lord, this fair green stone,
If so it pleases you——

Lion.   This emerald?
I'm glad you judge so well. Take it as pledge
Of my best friendship for your John and you.
[*To* LILIAS.] Now say, which shall be yours?

Lili.   None.
    I give thanks,
But I have need of nought.

Lion.   Need or no need,
Take one you must; a gold brooch serves as well
As a brass pin to make a kerchief fast.

Lili. The pin doth suit my state and the brooch not.
Sir, you must pardon me.

John.   'Tis right to have
Sense of your state, which truly is poor enough,
Being on us dependent, but to cast

Back on my lord his gifts is arrogance
That suits you least of all.
 Joan.   And is sure sign
Of a thankless churlish heart—not to take gladly
All things that come; and where she learned such ways
I know not—not from us.
 Lion.   Chide not too much.
Lilias, I pray you take—to pleasure me.
  Joan. [*Aside to* LILIAS.] The sapphire is the costliest.
  Lili. I will have
This, since I must.
 Lion.   What! this poor garnet clasp!
Meanest of all! You are too much a child
To be let choose. This sapphire, that, deep hid
In the earth, hath yet lain dreaming of Heav'n's blue—
The colour, as they say, of faithful love—
This shall be yours; and see, with mine own hand
I'll pin it in your kerchief. Why, how is't
You are so out of breath?

     Enter TOM TOD.

 Tom.   Lord Lionel!
 Lion. What! old Tom Tod! How goes it with old Tom?
 Tom. Ill, very ill. The cow has burst herself.
One might have thought a beast would have more sense
Than be so gluttonous.

Lion. Cheer up; we'll try
To find you comfort.
  Tom. The cow is not the worst;
My daughter sends me word my son-in-law
Has drunk himself to death; and I am left
With the little ones to keep—and the calf too.
  John. Then had you best keep all from following
Upon their parents' steps.
  Tom. And, sir, you know
I'm now your oldest tenant—the last left
Of all who at your christening drank the toast.
O shall I e'er forget how my good lord,
Your father, let me feel the weight of you?
Ay, and I plucked up heart to wipe my mouth,
And lay a sounding kiss upon your cheek—
Your cheek as soft and round as any peach.
I oft say 'tis not all who in their arms
Have held my lord, and kissed him on the cheek—
You have not, sir, yourself.
  Lion. O I know well
I have no older friend.
  Tom. And though 'tis true
Full many a thing you have been pleased to give,
I ne'er asked aught; and Master John of the Scales
Will tell you that no farthing of my rent
Was ever yet behind. But now, my lord,
These troubles others' faults have made for me
Have brought me here to ask you for a while
To show a little patience.

Lion.   Patience, man?
Ay, if you will, till the calf is grown a cow,
And your least grandchild wed. Look you, to-day
I am in haste, being yonder waited for;
Another time we'll talk; for present needs
Here is some gold—but stay! with the long way
I see you are tired and faint; get within doors,
And say I bade them feast you with the best.
And so for now farewell.   [*Exit.*
Tom.   And but to think
These arms once dandled him!
             [*Exit, towards the house.*
Joan.   Well, Lilias,
You have earned high wage to-day for little pains.
A goodly sapphire brooch, for which you ne'er
Have said so much as thanks.
    Lili.   I knew not how.
    Joan. You know not how to do aught that you
        should.
Your manners shame us in all companies;
And for my lord I think you keep your worst—
As crabb'd as if you bore him some hid grudge.
    John. And why you like him not 'tis hard to tell,
For sure to you he hath been kind enough,
Although it seems his kindness is forgot.
    Lili. O not forgot! Nay, I remember well,
And shall remember when all else is dim—
How, three years since, I came unto that door,
Footsore and weary, having in the world

But the orphan's weeds I wore, and that poor scrawl
My father, dying, wrote my uncle John;
And how you said you had not means to bear
More burdens than your own, and how again
I was going forth upon my unknown road,
When he o'erheard, and came, and bade me stay,
And told you all your spendings for my sake
Should be by him made up, and turned at once
Dark into light.
 Joan.   Here's a good memory!
Pity that where you think you owe so much
You let yourself be deemed a lumpish clod
That warms in the sunshine with no sense of thanks.
 Lili. O must he judge me thus?
 Joan.   How should he
  judge?
Girl, you have been a fool. There was a time
He looked on you, I fancied, with a favour
That might have ripened to I know not what;
But thereof must your peevish thankless ways
Have quite distasted him.
 John.   O a vile vice
Is ingratitude, the vilest vice that is.
Let us forget it if we can, and turn
To a theme more relishing. [*To* JOAN.] You ask me
  not
How the great bus'ness goes.
 Joan.   How?
 John.   To a wish.

Bills, and more bills, and ev'ry day more bills.
If this pace doth but hold, 'twill not be long
Ere you shall see your John a lord of the land,
The master of his master.

Joan. There's my heart!
And a rare lord thou'lt be, and one to make
The old ones look about. And when thou'rt lord,
I shall be lady, and go dressed in silk,
And never ask how much the yard?

John. I warrant,
And flaunt in blue and red and green and gold,
And chide at servants, and have delicate health,
Like any real lady.

Joan. Honey John!

John. My sugar-sweet! But while thou wait'st thy turn,
We are like to have another lady first.

Joan. What's this?

John. Nay, 'twill not hinder, rather help.
My lord to-day told me he had a mind
To woo for wife the Lady Geraldine;
But that is nought to us; her father's poor
As twice-skimmed milk; the wedding will but serve
To make more bills, and bring us faster on.

Joan. 'Twere hard indeed if aught should put you off,
You who have waited with such patient trust.

John. No fear. I've bided long, and borne full long

The niggard father's pinched ox-muzzling ways,
And then the patron airs of the thriftless son;
But now is my reward at hand and sure—
So Providence helps those that help themselves.

 Joan. And none e'er helped himself to more than
  you.
Come in, dear heart, and have a drink of ale,
And on the best chair shall you set your feet;
Your sweet face shines with all your toil and moil.

 John. Troth, a good comfortable wife thou art,
Whom 'twill be joy to make a lady of.

   [*Exeunt* JOHN *and* JOAN, *towards the house.*

 Lili. He to be wed! And yet a thousand times
I've told myself I must hear this one day;
And can I not believe? and learn to bear?
What is't to me? I that have hardly raised
Mine eyes to his, or spoke with him enough
To let him know I thank him; though in dreams
Oft—Ah! how oft—when sleep hath made me rich
And equal-born with him. But now ne'er more,
E'en in dreams now—ne'er more. O that word
  'wed'—
A happy word to some!   [*Weeps.*

    Enter HUBERT.

 Hub.   What have we here?
A pretty maid in tears, and all alone?
Then is there room for comfort and for me.
A kiss, my fair one, come. [*Laying hold of her.*

Lili.   Away! away!
Hub.   Nay, now, make haste; no time to be so coy;
There's company at hand.
Lili.   Help!

Enter LIONEL.

Lion.   On thy life
Let go that maiden.
Hub.   What! will you dare try
So high a voice with me?

Enter LORD *and* LADY FITZWATER, GERALDINE, SIR RUFUS ROLLESTONE, AMABEL, LETTICE, *and other Guests.*

Lady F.   How now! how now!
Hubert, what is't?
Hub.   Nought, but that here I found,
Weeping by herself, a pretty gardener wench,
And thought to give her comfort with a kiss,
When he came 'twixt us in as much of a storm
As though she were a queen and he her knight.
Lion.   What! weeping! my poor Lilias? was this so?
Sir, you have been to blame, and much to blame,
Yet shall you have her pardon, I doubt not,
Will you but let me tell her on your part
You are sorry.
Hub.   I to make excuse to her!

SCENE I.] *THE HEIR OF LINNE.* 113

Lady F. And more than that, good Hubert, would
 you do
To please my lord of Linne. [*Aside to* HUBERT.]
 What! are you mad?
Hub. Tell her whate'er you will.
Lion. Lilias, you hear;
Will you ask more than this?
Lili. O I ask nought—
Only your leave to go.
Lion. Nay, but not yet.
I will present you unto these my guests,
For some there are whom you perchance one day
May have to know. Friends, this is one who here
Should be with courtesy and kindness seen,
Both for herself, and since she is the niece
Of my old faithful servant, John of the Scales.
What! trembling still! thou hast been frighted sore.
 Geral. Or else maybe hath donned those pretty
 fears
As a becoming fashion.
 Lion. Why, in truth
They do become her well.
 Lady F. Now sure 'tis time
To turn unto concernments of more weight.
 Sir Ruf. [*Aside to* AMABEL.] More weight indeed
 if she be one of them.
 Lady F. And from us all, my lord, to give you
 thanks
For the pastime of to-day. O such a day!

Amab. In faith, a perfect day. Such pleasure 'twas
To see the wondrous coolness and strong hand
Of our dear Lady Geraldine bear off
So well deserved a prize.

Lett. O charming quite!
Though you, methinks, good sister, have no cause
To be ill pleased; that bracelet——

Amab. And who said
I was ill pleased? I'm ravished, overjoyed—
Such fire! such colour! [*Looking at her bracelet.*]
But my lord of Linne
In jewels hath the finest, rarest taste.

Sir Ruf. Ay, and in horses too, as I to-day
Have reason to be glad of.

Lady F. I'd not say
In jewels or in horses, but in all.
[*Aside to* LORD FITZWATER.] Have you no word?

Lord F. A marvellous rare taste!
Do but look round us; where will you see else
A park like this? such groups of trunks, such massings
Of light and shade in the foliage? And the house—
What lines! what symmetry of contrasted styles!
What depth! what breadth of meaning!

Lion. I am glad
You so approve, though neither did I plant
The trees, nor build the house.

Hub. As for the house,

'Twere well enough were this whole corner of it
Not spoiled by yonder hovel; to my mind
A lord's house is not lordly, elbowing
A battered barn.
 Amab.   That's scarce to be called fault
Which is so easy to be ta'en away.
 Sir Ruf. The site were good to build new stables
  on.
 Lett. Or a fair arbour twined with honey-suckle.
 Lord F. Or since perchance you have a reverence
For what is old—and truly in that wall
There is much feeling—it might be restored
So that you would not know it.
 Lion.   Ay, but, friends,
Of this can I do nought; that hut is mine,
And yet not mine.
 Sir Ruf. How so?
 Lion.   Of all you see,
'Tis the one thing that I can part with never,
And never lose, yet also the one thing
That I can have no use of.
 Lord F.   And the cause?
 Lion. Why, this. You know my father ere his death
Grew strange in many ways.
 Lord F.   I know—so strange,
He had no relish for the company
Of the best friends he had.
 Lion.   Well, of his ways
One of the strangest was that he was wont

To spend long days and nights shut up alone
In this old disused lodge, when he would suffer
Not me nor any near him. And how strong
Was his fancy for the place showed in his death
As much as in his life, for by his will
That crazy cot alone, of all I have,
I am restrained from power to give or sell
Or part with ever; yet from use thereof
Another clause debars me, which declares
It neither must be changed nor added to,
But left untouched in ev'ry beam and stone,
Nor yet by any lived in save by me,
And not by me until it shall become
The only home I have. When all else goes,
And I shall stand a beggar 'neath the sky,
That roof shall give me shelter. Fair provision
Against the perils of unthrift, is't not?

 Sir Ruf. A most sweet consolation for old age.
 Lord F. When all else goes! Too plainly now I see
That, as I feared, my poor friend's brain was touched.
 Lion. Indeed he was beset with the strangest whims.
Why, ere he died he even took distaste
'Gainst good old John of the Scales, and watched as though
To find him in a fault. Where's Lilias?
 [*Looking round for* LILIAS, *who has slipped away a moment before.*

Sir Ruf. A shy bird, good my lord, and flown
 away.
Lady F. She hath thought there was no further
 need of her—
As, in her place, most would.
 Lord F. Or feared perchance
The damp of the evening air.
 Lion. O pardon me;
I stay you here too long. Pray all, come in,
And these kind ladies of their charity
Shall give us help with dance and song to spend
The last dull remnant of a golden day.
Fair Lady Geraldine, the laws of war
Make you our queen to-night, so fit it is
That with your conqueror hand you grace your host.
 Geral. If 'tis the law, I must not say you nay,
Albeit too much you honour me.
  [LIONEL *leads her towards the house, the others
   following.*
 Amab. [*Aside to* LETTICE.] That's true.
I hate such singling-out.
 Lett. [*Aside to* AMABEL.] O in vile taste!
  [*Exeunt all into the house.*

 Enter TOM TOD, *carrying a basket, and* LILIAS.

 Lili. Take heed, I pray, in carrying, that the flagon
Chafe not the venison pasty. And remember,
The children's cakes are stowed between the folds
Of the napkin at the top.

Tom.   Bless your kind eyes,
And the kind heart that they are windows to!
I oft have said poor Tom in all the world
Hath but two friends ne'er tired of being friends,
And these two are, you and Lord Lionel.
    Lili. I and Lord Lionel! why, sure no two
So far apart were ever named in a breath.
    Tom. The names go well together in my prayers,
Where they are used enough to being joined.
    Lili. Be thanked for that!—I mean for having said
You pray for me. Beseech you do so still—
And for Lord Lionel, for well you know
He much deserves of you.
    Tom.   O that is so;
Heav'n's blessing be upon his comely face!
For sure a comelier never saw the sun—
And but to think I've held him in my arms,
And kissed his cheek! Not all can say as much;
You cannot, ha?
    Lili.   Nay, now, good master Tom,
How strangely do you talk! And see how fast
Night steals away the colour from all things;
You had best make haste.
    Tom.   Indeed I must be gone;
'Tis a long way, and my old bones are stiff.
Farewell, kind little mistress; may your heart
Ne'er feel desire but shall be filled as full—
As you have filled this basket.   [*Exit.*

Lili.   A kind wish!
But all too late.
  [*Music sounds from the house, the windows of
  which are now lighted up, the stage having for
  some time been growing gradually darker.*
                        Now is the dance begun;
He leads her forth by the hand, and 'neath his gaze
Her conscious eyes look down, yet see him still,
And trembling silent joy is o'er them both.
Ay, but they know not as I know what shadow
Of poverty and ruin lies in wait;
Could they but know, could she—O he might find
That ice can glow in the sun and yet be cold.—
How! am I glad? Ah! wretch! what! glad to think
He who hath done me nought but good must soon
Wander a landless beggar! O no! no!
So wicked am I not; Heav'n knows, to save him
From what must come, I'd even give my life.
But how? what can I do? how should I dare
In his presence lift my voice? and if I could,
What am I that my speech should find belief?
If I should say, 'That man you trust so much,
My uncle, for whose sake alone it is
I am fostered in this house, that man is false,'
How would he scorn my words! and me with them,
Base and unthankful more than e'en he deemed.
So must I wait and watch the ruin come,
And only strive with prayers.

Enter, from the house, LIONEL *and* GERALDINE.

                        Hark! voices! [*Seeing them*] Ah!
Where shall I fly? where hide?
    [*Ascends one or two of the steps leading up to the ruined cottage, and cowers from view behind the ivy-grown railing, but,* LIONEL *and* GERALDINE *drawing nearer, she has to steal up the staircase step by step until she reaches the balcony at the top, where she crouches down behind the balustrade.*

  Lion.   A fitter place
Than 'mid yon whirling foolish-laughing crowd
For speaking those first holy words of love
Thou hast giv'n me leave to say.
  Geral.   Ay, if but there
They miss us not, and wonder.
  Lion.   What of that?
All shall to-morrow learn what dear new rights
Thy answ'ring smile just now conferred on me.
  Geral.   I know not yet how I could be so bold.
  Lion.   Sit down, I pray, if thou wilt not disdain
To let me sit by thee.
  Geral.   Indeed, my lord,
I would not make you stand if you are tired.
    [*They seat themselves on the lowest step of the staircase.*
  Lion.   Give me thy hand.

Geral. Here, but what would you do
With aught so useless?
Lion. First commit on it
This most sweet theft, [*Kissing her hand*] and then for my offence
Pay penance with this ring, that, warm from pressing
My finger, now shall be the guard of thine.
Alack! I had forgot; too slender these
For aught of mine to fit them; but yet deign
To keep my pledge—see, put it on thy chain.
Geral. Or on your little finger there's a ring
Maybe would suit these foolish joints of mine—
Unless perchance it be a fair one's gift
You grudge to part with.
Lion. There's none fair save thee.
But for the world I would not give thee this;
This is a poisoned ring.
Geral. And you can say
'Tis poisoned, and yet wear it?
Lion. Ay, because
My father on his death-bed gave it me,
And bade me let it never from my hand,
But keep it safe as his best legacy.
Geral. How very strange your father must have been!
And then he told you there was poison in't?
Lion. He told me that if e'er the time should come
When I stood reft of fortune and of friends,

And all the light had faded from my sky,
I was to break this stone, and underneath
Should I find comfort.
 Geral.   O how horrible!
But I must wonder how your father's thoughts
Seemed to be brooding always on the image
Of you in want and ruin. There's no chance
Such dreams could e'er come true?
 Lion.   What! my dear
  love!
Can fear for me so ruffle thy smooth brow?
But let that cloud be lifted from thy heart,
Though me so much it flatters; for be sure,
Those fancies in my father were but bred
Of age and sickness; he hath told me oft
He left me richest lord in all the north;
So needst thou never fear to see me poor.
Art thou so glad?
 Geral. Mine own dear Lionel!—
Not that I reckon gold as more than dross.
 Lion. O well I knew! Now, fairest, hast thou set
My ring upon thy chain? I pray thee, haste
To make our contract whole by fett'ring me
With a ring of thine in turn. [*Taking a ring which she
  offers him.*] Too dainty-small
For my gross fingers; but yet, hanging here,
'Twill serve to mark my bondage. [*Fastens it to his
  chain.*
         And behold!

A happy sign ! as we plight troth the moon
From her silver-gated palace in the clouds
Looks forth, and shines full on the oak of Linne.
    [*Rising and pointing towards a tree.*
 Geral. The oak of Linne! thereof I ne'er have heard.
 Lion. What! knew you not we had an oak of Linne?
Ay, in good sooth, and a spirit of the oak,
The guardian of our race—sounds that not well?
Called the White Maid of Linne, or the Veiled Maid,
Which title best you like.
 Geral.   So ghostly both,
And haloed with romance, I could not choose.
There is a legend, sure, behind those names?
 Lion. Ay, that the lord of Linne who first built here
In ancient times his house had planned its site
In midst of a wood, where e'en then stood that oak,
And e'en then old, but marked by him to fall—
When lo! one night, the moon being full as now,
Walking alone among the trees to ponder
The fair proportions of his halls to be,
He heard his name called by a silver voice;
He looked, and saw amid the moonlit leaves
A form, all veiled in shining film, and hid,
Save for two arms, that made him long the more
To see the face, so white they were and fair—
As thine arms, love.

Geral.   Nay now, what foolishness!
Well, and what then?
    Lion.   Those arms so white and fair
Stretched towards him pleadingly, and through the
    veil
Sounded again the silver voice, and prayed
That he would suffer still that oak to stand,
Since she who spoke must live with it and die,
Her life with its life being made one by Fate.
    Geral. And like a gallant cavalier I see
He gave the fair her will.
    Lion.   Ay, nor had cause
To rue his yielding, for until his death
Was that veiled maid his friend, and oftentimes
Held converse with him 'neath the moon's pale rays,
And gave him counsel wise, and showed him secrets
Of the future and the past. And e'en to those
Of his blood that followed him, old stories say
She hath been known in the moonlight to appear
With words of timely teaching. But now men
Have grown so old in living that they see
No miracle in living or aught else,
And with the clang of new philosophies
Have scared the gracious visitant away.
    Geral. I see at least she hath not been so kind
As show herself to you.
    Lion.   And if to any
It should have been to me, for many a night
Here, when I was a boy, have I kept watch,

A truant from my pillow, till at last,
By cool—nay, icy-cold— considering,
I was constrained to think that the White Maid
Had ne'er been more than the pale gleam of the moon,
Shimmering in silver 'mong the swaying leaves.

Geral. You speak as though half sorry thus to think.

Lion. And so I am. 'Twere sweeter sure to deem
That here in this dull world we were o'erwatched
By a kind guardian spirit that at times
Deigned to be seen by us though through a veil,
And give us lessons of wisdom in our need—
So sweet that e'en now could I half believe.

Geral. I shall be jealous of your White Maid soon.

Lion. What said I? Nay, I wholly do believe;
Here is the proof, here my White Maid of Linne,
Who still will be my guide through life's rough ways;
And with no envious veil, but with red lips
Tempting a lover's kiss—as thus, and thus. [*Kissing her.*

Geral. Nay, pray you, pray you now. And hark, within
The music is at end; we shall be missed,
And greeted with who knows what foolish jests
And curious eyes. In pity take me back.
This poor heart flutters so.

Lion. I'll not deny
What thou thus pleadest for. Come, dear one, come.

[*Exeunt* LIONEL *and* GERALDINE *into the house.*
LILIAS *comes down from her hiding-place.*

Lili. How doth he shield and fold her round with
love !
O Heaven, of her blessings give her sense,
And let no cloud e'er fall athwart their joy.
No cloud ! alack ! the cloud hangs o'er them now,
Albeit by them unspied, and soon must break.
O might I speak and warn him ! Were but I
That white veiled maid he told her of! how soon
Would I put forth my wise protecting power
To counsel and to save the heir of Linne !
He would believe me then, and I, unseen
Behind my veil, could speak to him unabashed.
Were it but thus !—O what a thought was there !
If it could be !—What's this that sparkles so?
          [*Stooping.*
A ring ! a slender-fingered woman's ring !
This is the pledge she gave him ; then will he
Be back anon to seek it—and alone,
Since of such precious gift and of its loss
He would not lightly tell. He here alone !
And yonder, sleeping hushed beneath the moon,
The oak of Linne. It must be done and shall.
Now will I pay some of that debt I owe.
      [*Exit towards the house.*

Re-enter LIONEL.

Lion. Her first love-pledge, so sweetly given,
lost !
Could she but know, how careless should I seem

Of it and her alike! Yet am I not—
No, truly not—I love her with my heart,
Sure to the very height of all I dreamed
That love could ever be. So fair! so kind!
Who could wish more than I have found in her?
Or even to himself imagine more,
On this side Heaven?—Where should be that ring?
> [*As he wanders about looking on the ground,* LILIAS,
> *veiled, glides from behind the trunk of the oak-
> tree.*

Lili. Lionel, lord of Linne.

Lion. Who is't that calls?—
O thou long waited for, is't thou at last?—
Or else am I perchance but jested with?

Lili. No jest is this, but thy best friend thou seest,
Who what she owes thy race would now pay back
With needed counsel. But ere more be said
Take up thy ring, thy Geraldine's first gift,
That at thy foot lies shining.

Lion. O 'tis so!
> [*Stooping for the ring, then kneeling.*

Now do I find thy truth, immortal one,
And humbly thus adore.

Lili. Since with such awe
Thou bendest to my voice, let now its precepts
Find in thy heart like rev'rence. To no man
Give too much trust, but let thyself be he
Who in thine own concernments hath most part
Of knowledge both and guidance; in thy house

And inmost counsels thou dost cherish now
A traitor that doth wrong thee.
Lion.   O and who?
Can any be so base?
Lili.   Take thou thyself
Governance of thine own, and thou shalt both
Discover and defeat. Yet one thing more
It needs to save thee—this; in all thou spendest
Count what is left behind, lest thou with giving
The means of giving waste, and thy to-day
On thy to-morrow feed. No store too great
For the gluttony of unthrift to swallow up,
And thine to its end is nearer than thou knowest.
Dost heed my words?
Lion.   O with religious ear.
Lili. Take then my blessing with thee, heir of Linne,
And keep my counsels still. Be frugal, wise,
And trust no man too much by night or day,
So shalt thou thrive.
    Lion. [*Bowing down his head reverentially.*] I worship and obey.

                                       [*The Curtain falls.*

END OF ACT I.

ACT II.

'They ranted, drank, and merry made,
　　Till all his gold it waxèd thin;
And then his friends they slunk away,
　　They left the unthrifty heir of Linne.

ACT II.

SCENE I.

A Hall for dancing.

LILIAS *and* JOAN *discovered, the former arranging garlands on the wall, the latter entering with a basket of flowers.*

Joan. Here are more flowers to finish the festoons—
And best make haste; else will the company
Come in to dance, and find you at your task.
 Lili. 'Tis well-nigh done. Strange that our lord should care,
Night after night, for revels such as these.
 Joan. Not strange at all for empty heads to dance;
No brains need fear no jolting. Much more strange
'Twas when he talked to my good man this morn
Of the need of thrift. That, if you like, was strange.
But the whim will pass as others. Well, well, girl,
Keep to your work. Thrift and frugality!
Fine new words these! And where he had them from
I cannot understand.   [*Exit.*
 Lili.   Yea, but I can.

Kind Heav'n, if thou hast let me do him good,
My prayers from this day forth must all be thanks.

Enter LIONEL.

O pardon—I have finished. [*Going.*
   Lion.   Nay, I pray,
Be not so scared. Are you afraid of me,
That when I come you are always finishing?
   Lili. Afraid of you, my lord! wherefore afraid?
   Lion. 'Tis what I ask. And hark you, Lilias,
I've news for you to-day that I must beg
Good wishes for. You see before you one
Made very happy with a promised wife—
The Lady Geraldine. Knew you of this?
   Lili. I knew, my lord.
   Lion.   And will not wish me joy?
   Lili. O yes; indeed, indeed I wish you joy.
   Lion. I well believe. Remember, little maid,
That whether I be wed or not shall make
No difference to you.
   Lili.   O none at all.
   Lion. I mean, you and your uncle and his wife
Shall with a lord and lady still live here
As you have lived till now with but a lord—
Save that your uncle's post shall be henceforth
Of greater ease and leisure, for I look,
When I am wed, to fill my idle hours
With taking of mine own concerns more charge
Than yet I have, and being mine own steward.

Lili. Not before then, my lord?
Lion.   O 'twill be soon.
For your good uncle have no fear meanwhile;
Till then in sooth I cannot. Shall a lover
Have time for reck'nings and for castings-up—
Save of his eyes unto his fair one's face?
You ought to be more learnèd in love's lore,
And shall some day, I hope; a better wish
I could not give you, child. What! in such haste?
  Lili. Ay, please, my lord.
  Lion.   I will not stay you more.
                                 [*Exit* LILIAS.
Strange, how her voice seems as it were to stir
A sleeping memory that yet wakes not!

                Enter HUBERT.

What! Hubert! Welcome always, in your own
And your fair sister's right.
  Hub.   I thank you well.
Can you spare leisure for some private speech
Before the dance begins?
  Lion.   Whate'er you will
You may command me in.
  Hub.   There is in truth
A little favour——
  Lion.   Say.
  Hub.   Why, as you know,
We are brothers now.
  Lion.   So my kind stars have ruled.

Hub. And, being such, I feel it is your due,
Almost a debt I owe you, not to hide
You can from ruin save me if you will.
   Lion. O how? What ruin?
   Hub.   Ruin for the want
Of what to you will seem so slight a thing
I could half shame to tell; thirty-nine thousand—
Call them for roundness, forty thousand—crowns.
Well?
   Lion. Forty thousand crowns!
   Hub.   The use of them,
Say for three years. Nay, you should have my bond,
All in due form.
   Lion.   O all in form, no doubt.
But forty thousand crowns!
   Hub.   I see how 'tis;
I have offended you. I know of late
My troubles may have made me seem perchance
A little crabb'd and sullen.
   Lion.   No in faith!
No more than always—'tis not that, I swear.
[*Aside.*] How would she counsel here? [*Aloud.*] Tell
    me then, Hubert,
How came you in this need?
   Hub.   O well I knew
You would be gen'rous still—and will repay you
With the candid truth. A month ago, at cards—
By no fault of mine own, but sheer ill-luck—
I lost the money, and since, as it fell out,

I had not at the time enough at hand
To acquit myself at once, I was constrained
To ask a month's delay, and now the month
Is at an end; more simple nought could be.
    Lion. Longer they will not wait?
    Hub.   Nay, but make
      threat
They will proclaim me unto all the world.
I have letters here your blood would boil to read—
Telling me to my face I cannot pay;
And truly but for your great kindness now,
I see not how I could.
    Lion.   Would not your father——
    Hub. My father, might he know of this, would
      ne'er
Speak word to me again. I could bear that,
If he would help—but you may pluck the hairs
Out of a bald man's pate as easily
As money from my father. Without you,
I should be now dishonoured and undone,
Banned from the company of gentlemen,
And cards, and sports, and all.
    Lion. [*Aside.*]   Dishonoured—he!
'Twould break his sister's heart. [*Aloud.*] Not a
      word more;
The money's yours, and to your hands shall pass
Within the instant. Do but stay for me
In my private closet yonder, while I bid
My steward unlock his coffers.

Hub.   I shall rest
All my life long your debtor.
  Lion.   So I know.
That way—I'll follow soon.   [*Exit* HUBERT.]   What
    ho! Who's there?

Enter a SERVANT.

Sirrah, go straight to Master John of the Scales.
Say for a present purpose I have need
Of forty thousand crowns, which I would have him
At once bring hither.   [*Exit* SERVANT.]   Nay, with
    mine own self
And mine own pleasures must my thrift begin,
Not with my friend in his extremest need,
My friend, and brother of my plighted wife;
This can she ne'er have meant—that spirit pure
Who hath me in her keeping, and will lead me
To wiser and to better.   Some would say
That what I saw last night, and what I heard—
Yea, e'en that heav'nly voice, that in mine ear
So soft-compelling rings—was but a dream;
Yet surely 'twas no dream; no more a dream
Than all things fair and fleeting, than the sweep
Of the wind athwart a field of golden grain,
Or the passing breath of roses, or the warble
Dying as 'tis born from the nightingale's sweet
    throat,
Or the faint thrills that sometimes in men's hearts
Open and shut the gates of Paradise—

All fairest, soonest o'er, and for no price
To be commanded back, and yet not dreams.

Enter JOHN OF THE SCALES, *with a wallet.*

O my good John, thanks for this diligence;
You have the money yonder?
 John.   Ay, my lord;
In bonds and gold just forty thousand crowns.
They told me you thereof had instant need.
 Lion. So have I, or so hath at least the friend
Whom they are purposed for. Give hither quick;
He waits e'en now.
 John.   Then from your hands, my lord,
They will be parted with to his at once?
 Lion. Ay; wherefore not?
 John.   No reason that I know.
I did but ask because, when you with him
Shall quite have done your bus'ness, I would crave
Upon a poor concernment of mine own
A little of your leisure.
 Lion.   And 'twere hard
If you, so ready always at my call,
Should not sometimes find me at yours. Wait here;
I'll come anon. [*Aside.*] My life on't, 'tis not he
I am bid beware of.   [*Exit.*
 John.   Sooner than I thought—
Those forty thousand crowns to me are worth
A month of wedding feasts and wedding bills.
Well, well, 'tis not my part now to have qualms;

As he has made his bed so must he lie,
And so must I on mine; and if henceforth
My bed is soft, why, I have made it soft
By working early and late, and all day long
Fetching and carrying for a purse-proud fool,
Who yawned while I was toiling. Now that's done,
And I, who yet have only licked my fingers
At others' dishes, may set mouth myself
Unto mine own, and never heed who sees.

Re-enter LIONEL.

Lion. Well, John, what would you tell me? some
   good news?
For truly you were chuckling to yourself
Like a pleased pigeon.
   John. [*Aside.*]   A pert cub! to try
His sauciness on his betters! [*Aloud.*] Is my lord
Quite sure he is at leisure, and hath finished
That bus'ness with his friend?
   Lion.   I had nought to do
But give the money, and have given it.
   John. [*Aside.*] Once given ne'er comes back.
   [*Aloud.*] Sir, as I said,
'Tis on a little matter of mine own
I now must trouble you. You will remember
Those five-and-twenty thousand crowns wherewith
I had the happiness, a twelvemonth past,
Of minist'ring to your conveniency
In the way of loan—my little all, my lord,

Hard earned by a life of toil, but willingly
Adventured in your service.
    Lion.   O I know—
Some moneys that you said had to be paid
Just ere the rents fell due, and you till then
Offered to lend them; but methought long since
You would have made this good.
    John.   Nay, I was loth
To do aught unseasonable. But, my lord,
It chances now that I myself am called
To make a payment to a creditor,
The stoniest-hearted fellow that e'er lived.
So for those five-and-twenty thousand crowns
I am constrained to ask.
    Lion.   Why, take them then;
You are keeper, as you know, of all my store.
    John. Of all, my lord?
    Lion.   You know it. Pay your-
        self.
    John. Alas! but with that sum I gave you now
Your money-chest is drained.
    Lion.   What say you there?
Is this your stewardship? How! for a day
To leave me bare!
    John.   Will not your lordship please
To pay me back that money that you owe?
    Lion. Pay! and you say my money-chest is drained!
    John. I'm sorry much, my lord, but I must seek
Means to be paid, or shall be quite undone.

Lion. Go to the town, and borrow in my name,
And take your money back with usury,
But be no more my steward.
  John. [*Aside.*]   So! dismissed!
[*Aloud.*] You speak, my lord, of borrowing in the town,
But were you known there for a borrower,
You who already owe so much, the news
Would bring on you a flock of unpaid bills
As thick as locusts, which would eat all up
That in your house seems yours, both goods and
    jewels.
  Lion. Were this but true, thou wouldst not dare to
    tell—
And yet, if false, e'en less.
  John.   I wish, my lord,
You would consider how I may be paid;
'Tis ruin for me else.
  Lion.   Then hast thou wrought
Thy ruin for thyself.
  John.   I'd fain hope not.
There was a bond, my lord, a little bond,
Which when you took that loan from me you signed—
Whereby you pledged yourself to pay in full,
After a twelvemonth's use, within the space
Of four-and-twenty hours from the time I asked;
Or, failing, should your house and lands be mine.
. Now, though 'twould grieve me infinitely——
  Lion.   Slave!
You told me when I signed 'twas but a form.

L

John. And who could dream 'twas other than a
    form
With one who, like your lordship, seemed to live
By spending, as more common men by food?
But since indeed that form has come to be
The only safeguard of my little all,
'Twould show in me a bad rebellious mind
Not to be thankful.
    Lion. And a spirit came
To warn me 'gainst thee, and I heeded not!
Too used unto thy fat familiar face
To guess it could be signboard to a heart
Of such foul difference from other men's.
Should I not now be doing to the world
A good turn if I crushed thy vile life out?
                                              [Seizing him.
    John. What! would you do me hurt? A poor
    old man,
Grey in your service! Help!
    Lion. O get thee gone!
I shame to have touched thee. *[Pushing him away.*

                    Enter JOAN.

    Joan. Why, what have we here?
Panting, sweet John! How's this? what hath he
    done?
    John. Shaken my teeth together for nought else
But that I told him I must be constrained
To put in force that bond whereof you wot,

To save the little earnings of my life
From being puffed and blown away by the wind
Of his great fortune's fall.

Joan.   What! then the time
Is come I shall be lady?

Lion.   Ay, a time,
I see, that hath been watched and waited for.
Base villain!—O fear nought; I'll not defile
My fist on such as thou.

Joan.   Defile! heyday!
On worse defilement you may chance to light.

John. Nay, let him think of that e'en as he will.
My lord, ere putting on me these hard words,
Were it not best examine for yourself,
And, if you can, lay finger on my fault?
In the steward's chamber will you see my books
Laid open to your view, nor do I fear
You'll find a groat there not accounted for.

Lion.   I'll swear to that; thou art too false thyself
Not to take care thy books at least are true.
But come, and show; 'tis right mine eyes should see
The proofs that prove me beggar and thee knave.

[*Exeunt* LIONEL *and* JOHN.

Joan. These be great airs! And he without a rood
Of land to call his own! If there's a thing
In the world I hate, 'tis folk that think themselves
Better than other folk, while all the time
Those others know 'tis they that are the best.

Enter LILIAS.

Lili. O what hath chanced? Just now our lord passed by
As pale and wan and little like himself
As his own corse might look; and with him went
My uncle John, following his master's steps
Slowly, as one half scared. Is there ill news?

Joan. The news is, child, that you mistake to call
The lord of Linne, or any lord that is,
Your uncle's master, for of all things here
Your uncle's self is master—or would be
Except that I am mistress.

Lili.   Is this so?

Joan. Ay, is it, and his lordly lordship knows,
Spite of big ways and words. Well, have you not
A tongue to say you are glad?

Lili.   So white and wild!
O fear you not whereto he may be driven
By prick of unaccustomed misery?
Perchance to lay upon himself rash hands.

Joan. That I know not; 'tis all his own affair;
Better than lay them on my poor dear John.
Cold-hearted that you are!

Lili.   That poisoned ring!
O me! how near and with what tempting ease
In this his darkest hour doth death invite!

Joan. Be't as you will; my time serves not to wait
Till you have done with mumbling. I must go

And sort my wardrobe o'er, and see how best
I may array myself to meet my guests,
The lords and ladies now beneath my roof. [*Exit.*
　Lili. Death in so small a compass and so near!
Prescribed by his own father! O bad father,
Blot upon nature! who could thus foresee
His son's dire need, yet 'gainst that bitter time
Provide nought else than death. Nought else than
　　death?
Nay, but that disused lodge—was not that left
To be provision for him in his want?
'When I shall stand a beggar 'neath the sky,
That roof shall give me shelter.' Thus he said,
And laughed to think the will had so decreed.
Why then, his father meant him not to die!
Peace, foolish heart, peace—let me think. His father
With his last breath bestowed on him that ring,
And said if e'er his sky was quite o'ercast
He was to break the stone, and underneath
Should he find comfort. Why not life and hope
Rather than death? surely a likelier pledge
To be bequeathed by a father to a son.
O that I had but some authority
To counsel him! and bid him break that stone,
I being at his side, to watch, and dash
The poison from his hand if poison 'twere.
Might it not be I could bring this to pass?
Perchance. O aid me, Heav'n, and comfort him.
　　　　　　　　　　　　　　[*Exit.*

Enter LORD *and* LADY FITZWATER, HUBERT, GERALDINE, SIR RUFUS ROLLESTONE, AMABEL, LETTICE, *and other Guests, Musicians following.*

Lady F. What bus'ness 'tis that keeps him I know not,
But unto me he sends expressly word
His absence for a while must in no wise
Be hindrance to your pleasures, or put off
The looked-for dance. So in his name I pray you
Choose partners and begin. Music, strike up.
[*They dance.*

Enter LIONEL, JOHN OF THE SCALES *following.*

Lion. Break off—let silence be. Your pardon, friends;
But I have that to say which till 'tis said
Burns in my throat.
  Lady F. Alas! my lord, what is't?
  Lion. And yet as hard to tell as keep untold—
You being all my friends, to whom my griefs
Are even as your own.
  Lady F. O but yet tell.
  Hub. We'll strive our best to bear.
  Sir Ruf. We will be strong.
  Lion. Know then, a beggar stands before you here—
A landless, houseless beggar.
  Lady F. What means this?
O now I see—a jest.

Lord F.   Faith, a good jest.
Sir Ruf.   Or would be good if 'twere not beggarly.
Hub.   When next you try the appetite of belief,
Offer a smaller mouthful.
    Lion.   Have you ne'er
Heard a voice speak from a sad heart before,
That now you know it not? I say again
I am a beggar, out of land and goods
Tricked by yon villain, who of all you see
Is master and disposer.
    John.   'Tis quite true,
Dear lords and ladies, though so strange it seems—
True, I mean, I am master; which, I take it,
Is the point of chief concern.
    Lion.   Ay, true, all true.
He hath spent, and let me spend, till from my store
The last round coin hath rolled (surely made round
To roll the easier); and, more than this,
Hath tied my hands so to my sides with debt
I cannot reach them forth for timely aid,
And must stand by and see a bond enforced
That gives to him the house and lands of Linne.
    John.   Yes, if before this hour to-morrow night
Those five-and-twenty thousand crowns you owe
Be not paid back in full—my little all.
    Lion.   Thus stands it, friends. You see, a desp'rate
        case.

[*A pause, during which the Guests look at each other,*
                                    and whisper.

[*Aside.*] Poor girl, poor love; I dare not lift my eyes
To where she is, as one who stabs himself,
Yet turns away from looking on the wound.
[*To* AMABEL, *who stands near him.*] Tell me, how
 fares the Lady Geraldine?
 Amab. I will go comfort her. O my sweet friend!
 Lett. Need I say how I pity?
 Geral.   You need not—
Nor pity one who pities not herself.
 Lion. [*Aside.*] I knew not how she loved me, or
 how true
She spake, saying that gold to her was dross.
Come, for her sake I will be strong as she.
[*Aloud.*] Your silence, friends, well shows you think
 the time
Too short for help to reach me.
 Lord F.   Why indeed
I see not how, in four-and-twenty hours——
To be quite plain with you, as sure I am
You wish us to be plain, I cannot think
You have been wholly prudent.
 Hub.   Rankest folly
To put such trust in others! 'Tis so easy
To keep account oneself of what one owes.
 Sir Ruf. Had you been earlier open with your
  friends!
There would have then been time for us to give
Advice that might have saved.
 Lion.   But now, I see,

'Tis all too late for friendship's self to help—
And trust me, though time served you to redeem
My lands, as well I know you fain would do,
I ne'er had suffered you to have your will
At any peril of your own grave loss.
The folly hath been mine, and mine must be
The paying of the forfeit.
    Lord F.   On my word,
A noble spirit.
    Sir Ruf.   From my lord of Linne
I looked for nothing less, yet must admire.
    Lion. And now that of my state you know the
        worst,
You next shall learn my hopes, the arms wherewith
I look to vanquish Fortune; for be sure
While I have friends—or others peradventure,
Called by a dearer name—who still will deign
To wish me well, I'll wrestle for their sake
Till I have slain my troubles or they me,
Yea, strive to tame disaster for my slave
To help me to new wealth, which I'll go forth
Into the world to conquer with the sword
Of love and hope.
    Lord F.   An excellent resolve!
    Sir Ruf. Wherein all our best wishes shall be
        yours.
    Lion. Thanks. If those wishes have borne fruit
        or not
Before three years are over shall you know;

For three years being ended, with no sight
Or news of me, conclude me either dead
Or of my hopes fall'n short, and look no more
To see me in your midst. And thou, who once
Wert to have been the sunshine of my home,
Think thyself free, when those three years are done,
To make bright with thy smiles another's hearth;
Longer I would not have thy fair young life
Wasted with bootless waiting.

Lady F.   But my lord,
Since to my daughter still you seem to ascribe
Part in your fortunes, you will pardon me
If I should ask you what the surety is
For their so speedy mending.

Lion.   Chiefly, madam,
Strong heart and hands, by love made stronger.

Lady F.   Ah!

Lion. The gold I hope one day to dower her with
Is now stored up in that new fairer world
Mariners tell us of beyond the west,
The treasure-house of earth, rich with the glow
Of million sunsets—there will I go seek
My second fortune, or, it may be, chance
To find it on the seas, where Spanish galleons
Crowd sail at sight of the smallest English bark.

Lady F. A little scattered, sir, it seems to lie.

Lion. Not long ago I held discourse with one
Who in those lands and waters of the west
Had made himself from poor in brief space rich,

And who so took my ear his prisoner
With things he told me—of balm-breathing groves
Where birds like jewels sparkle in and out,
And many-coloured skies that blend and change
With the blushing hills their blushes—then again
Of the crash of oak 'gainst oak, and steel 'gainst steel,
And the scared cry of Spaniards to their saints,
And, following soon, the full-voiced English cheer
Telling of victory, and good gold won
From use of foreign foes—with things like these
He so ensnared my fancy that well-nigh
He made me wish my fortune still to seek.
 Sir Ruf. [*Aside.*] A modest wish, soon granted.
 Lion.   He I speak of—
A wealthy burgher now—a few years since
Had only in the world his own stout heart,
And a poor patrimony of no more
Than some two thousand crowns, but these enough
To equip and man the bark that made him heir
Of far-off Indian kings and Spanish dons.
Now I, you see, am strong, and of a spirit,
I trust, to dare as much as any dare;
So with two thousand crowns I hope to make
My fortunes equal his. These still I lack,
But shall not long, I know, when once I say
That of my friends I will not shame to ask
A petty loan that will not do them hurt.
Which of you all will lend two thousand crowns?
Or give; since it may be that death, belched up

By angry seas, or slung by foeman's hand,
Will make my bond a mock. Which of you? speak.
　　　　　　　　　　　　　　　　　　[*A pause.*
I see you think it is for me to choose
Whom I will have for helper, and in truth
Where I know all to be so much my friends,
By making choice of one I need not fear
To give the rest offence. Hubert Fitzwater,
To you in this great need I bring my suit,
Both since you are my brother, and because
I did you lately a good turn, which now
I should be churlish if I gave you not
Occasion to requite.

　　Hub.　　　　　What! taunt me, sir,
With favours past? I have just now at hand
No more than what for present use I need;
But let me say, if aught could make me fling
Your favours back into your teeth, 'twere this.

　　Lion. I do confess that when I asked of you
Most gravely I mistook; yet pray believe,
To taunt you I meant not. Sir Rufus Rollestone,
In the shrill-voiced hunting-field, and at the board
Where wine makes warm, you long have been my friend,
Nor now that sport and feast for me are done
Will be aught other. Those two thousand crowns
Whereon I build my hopes I ask of you,
Nor shame·to ask.

　　Sir Ruf.　　　　Of me! Upon my life,
More sorry am I than I well can say,

But I have paid away of late such sums——
That new estate I bought—and then some wine
I've just laid down—and, to confess the truth,
I scarce can see my way——
   Lion.   Yet in your place
Methinks I could have found one. Nay, not now—
Although you offered now, I would not take.
   Sir Ruf. I offer not; would only that I could
In justice to myself.
   Lion.   Will none else speak?
Not one among them all?   O now I find
What I knew not before—a poor man's friends
In justice to themselves must all be poor.
Why then, my Lord Fitzwater, unto you,
Whom I thought not to trouble, must I turn,
You who perchance less easily can spare
Than some of those, who will not.
   Lord F.   And who said
I could not spare? you take upon yourself
To speak strange things. It doth indeed fall out
That at this moment—most unhappily—
At this especial moment——
   Lady F.   At this moment
He hath to think of the welfare of his child,
So can do nought to help the hopes of one
Whose suit he favours not, and doth forbid.
Is it not so, my lord?
   Lord F.   'Twas even thus
I was about to say.

Lion.　　　　　　　You would deny me
All chance of winning her?
　　Lady F.　　　　　　Most absolutely,
As a suitor quite unfit.
　　Lord F.　　　　　O quite unfit.
　　Lion.　But your denial, sir, and, madam, yours,
I will not take ; 'tis she, and only she,
Whose sentence I will stand by.　Geraldine,
Betrothed, belovèd, speak ; will you not wait
A poor three years, to see if for your sake
I cannot force from Fortune's hand as much
As will, with my great love, make up a tribute
That, at your feet laid, your love will not scorn ?
Answer, and for the battle give me strength.
　　Geral.　My parents have for me made answer,
　　　　sir,
Whereby, as is my duty, I abide.
　　Lion.　Because it is your duty, not your will?
Nay, then, if still you love me, I have right
To claim you still for mine, my bride, my queen,
Whom in the citadel of my love I'll hold
'Gainst all the opposing world.　That duty's none
Which bids you break your heart.
　　Geral.　　　　　　　O but I hope
My heart is framed less weakly than you deem,
And since you thus constrain me to speak plain,
I tell you, sir, I can as easily
Put from my heart one that in false disguise
Hath sought to enter there, as from my person

This token of my all too simple trust
And his deceit.
> [*Disengages a ring from her chain, and throws it down.* LIONEL *mechanically does the same, then looks round, as one bewildered.*]

Lion. They have the faces still
Of men and women. I should say I dreamed,
But that of men and women I ne'er thought
So ill that I could dream such things as these.
Now am I taught, and see that men and women
Are only devils loosed awhile on earth
For holiday, and making masquerade
In hired-out scraps and shreds of virtuousness,
Put on and off like clothes, save that the clothes
Are better fitting. Hence from out my sight,
Ye hideous rout, nor bring my house to shame
With the nakedness of your vile souls laid bare.

Sir Ruf. Is it of us he speaks?

Lady F. He must be mad.

Lion. Away, I say; pollute not more my roof
With steam of your false breaths; they turn me sick.
How! still you stay? O I well-nigh forgot
What you, I see, remember—that no more
I'm master in this house; you are right, quite right;
Here is your host, to whom such guests as you
Will, I doubt not, be welcome.

John. Ay indeed,
Kind lords and ladies, will you but vouchsafe
Your gracious presence for a few brief days.

'Twould make me proud for ever; and the same
I know that I may say for my poor wife,
Would it but please you so to honour us.

  Lord F. Very well worded, and well mattered too.
Now there's a man who for his state in life
Hath always seemed stamped with a certain stamp.

  Lady F. For me, though none, I hope, more loth
   than I
To meddle with the bounds 'twixt high and low,
Still I would say that when it once hath chanced
One of the common sort hath raised himself
Above the common sort, it then becomes
A kind of duty to encourage him.

  Sir Ruf. So say I too. Good man, we'll be your
   guests
As long as it shall please you.

  John.   O I know
Not half so long as that can you withdraw
From your own sphere your light to shine in mine;
But yet a little while, a few brief days,
I hope you will not grudge me, and I'll strive
My best to be content. [*To* LIONEL, *who is laughing.*]
  And you, my lord,
Whom I am glad with all my heart to see
In such a mirthful vein, if you will please
Bestow on me your honoured company,
You'll find a welcome wait, and may indeed
Command me in all reasonable things.
No man shall say that I, when I was up,

Forgot you once were up and I was down;
Nor shall you ever see me take offence
At being thereof reminded.
 Lord F.   A good fellow,
With a simple humble heart.
 John.   I see my lord
Holds me in too much scorn to be my guest;
Be't even so. Yet truly for to-night
None but your lordship's self is here the host,
Since of this house for four-and-twenty hours
You still are master.
 Lion.   All my need, I hope,
Of house, or food, or fire, or aught besides,
In four-and-twenty hours will be at end.
Begin to play your part of master now;
It doth divert me much. Where else in the world
Could such host match such guests? Why, anywhere,
In ev'ry part beneath the sun where dwells
The hind-leg-walking beast. It seems not yet
I have learned my lesson quite, but soon I shall.
Out on you! out! O how my very soul
Doth heave with hate and loathing of you all,
You swine, you wolves, you compounds of things vilest
On earth and under earth, you serpents, devils—
Nay, worse yet, men and women.
 Lady F. [*To* JOHN.]   Pray you, sir,
Whither shall we withdraw? It is not fit
Our ears should be so sullied.

M

John.   Faith, 'twere best
For him and us to leave him to himself.
This way, sweet ladies, this way, honoured sirs;
By me and my poor wife you will find spared
No pains to make you welcome.
    Lady F.   Honest friend!
            [*Exeunt all except* LIONEL.
    Lion.   I said I hated them, but I have cause
As much to hate myself. I am man too,
Made of the self-same flesh and blood as they.
O shame not to be borne—nor shall it long;
There is a way to 'scape. Father, wise father,
How well you knew the world you left me in,
When, as your last and richest legacy,
You gave me means to quit it! Yet perchance
Not the best means, or surest; by my side
I have another friend that might methinks
Deal quicker—sharper at the first maybe,
But who will use no dallying with my pain,
Who will be brief if bidden to be brief.
Come forth, thou trusty one.
        [*He unsheathes his sword. At the same time, un-
            noticed by him, a curtain is drawn at the back
            of the stage, showing a window standing open,
            with a moon-lit garden beyond. In the opening
            appears* LILIAS, *veiled.*
                            Ay, in this point
A med'cining virtue dwells that hath not lost
Its strength by keeping—sharp and swift and sure,

If driv'n but deep enough, by an arm well nerved
With hate and utter scorn, such scorn as mine
For one who would have been like all his kind
Save for his greater folly.   Friend, prepare ;
I never gave thee yet man's blood to drink,
But now thou shalt be red with it all thy length,
Though I shall not behold.
  Lili. [*Who has glided forward till she stands almost
  at his side.*]   Put up thy sword.
  Lion.   Spirit !
  Lili.   Put up thy sword.
  Lion.   See, I obey ;
But wherefore heed me ?
  Lili.   Swear that ne'er again
Thou give this purpose entrance in thy soul,
And shame to think it hath been ever there.
Thy life is not thine own, since on thyself
Thou hast conferred it not, and is but held
In trust for the giver, whom in rifling it
Thou foully dost betray.
  Lion.   A trust by me
Not asked for, and imposed without my will.
  Lili.   Ay, but by thee accepted since imposed
More times than thou canst number.   Thou hast ne'er
Held up thy face rejoicing to the glow
Of morning sun or evening, or been glad
To feel the west wind's kisses on thy cheek,
Or joyed in the breath of sweet flowers after rain,
But that thou even then didst bind thyself

To bear life's ills with patience, as with pleasure
Thou didst receive its goods. Swear that ne'er more
Thou'lt seek to make rebellion 'gainst the bond
By thee so oft contracted.

Lion.   Spirit, I swear,
Since thou dost bid me, though thou bidst me break
The counsel that my dying father gave.

 Lili. And canst thou think thy dying father counselled
Self-murder to his son?

 Lion.   This ring——

 Lili.   That ring
He gave thee, saying that behind the stone
Thou shouldst find comfort in thy darkest need.
Hast thou yet sought it there?

 Lion.   No. But what comfort
Save death——

 Lili.   Obey him. Break the stone and look.
 [LIONEL *strikes his ring with the hilt of his sword.*
Well, and thou findest——

 Lion.   A small folded square
Of yellow parchment.

 Lili.   Open heedfully;
What see'st thou?

 Lion.   Some few lines of writing.

 Lili.   Read.

 Lion. [*Reading.*] *I left thee foolish, now I find thee wise,*
Schooled in the school of the world with tears and sighs;

Now therefore, son, I trust thee with the store
I feared to leave to thy untaught hands before.
Hie to the hut forlorn that still is thine,
And dig, and thou shalt see a treasure shine
Richer than all thou hast lost, nor lost in vain,
Since now thy loss turns doubly to thy gain.
Mine eyes read well the words, but scarce I know
If my understanding right interprets them.

   Lili. It doth—that thou art rich again, and great;
Bow down thy head in thanks to gracious Heaven
That plucks thee back from death to better life.

      [LIONEL *holds down his head, covering his face with*
         his hands. LILIAS *slowly retreats towards the*
         window. When she has reached it, he looks up.

   Lion. And to thee, spirit—thee, Heav'n's messenger.
O leave me not; test first my thankfulness
With what command thou wilt, and I'll obey.

   Lili. Make of thy second wealth a wiser use
Than of thy first; be happy, and farewell.   [*Exit.*

   Lion. Happy she bids me be! Ay, if I can—
If not, at least avenged on the race of man.
                          The Curtain falls.

END OF ACT II.

ACT III.

'And he pulled forth the bags of gold,
　And laid them down upon the board;
All woe-begone was John of the Scales,
　So vexed he could say never a word.'

ACT III.

SCENE I.

A Banqueting-room.

JOHN *and* JOAN *discovered, presiding at opposite ends of a supper-table, round which are assembled* LORD *and* LADY FITZWATER, HUBERT, GERALDINE, SIR RUFUS ROLLESTONE, AMABEL, LETTICE, *and the other Guests —Servants in attendance.*

Lord F. Since I must give the toast, friends, here
      it is,
And in its honour fill your glasses high.
To our worthy honest host and his good dame
Health and long life.
  All.   Health and long life! [*All drink.*
  John.   Too much!
Such favour to myself and my poor wife
I know not how to thank you for.
  Joan.   John.
  John.   Love
  Joan. You need not always now say your poor
      wife;

To make us worse than what we are is scarce
Good manners to our guests.

John.   Well, it may be
Not now so very poor—not in one way;
But all too poor in words, the silver change
Of the golden gratitude stored up within.

Lord F.   Very well put.

John.   O we both know our place,
Both I and my poor ——

Joan.   John.

John.   I and my wife—
And know what honour you bestow on us,
You that are lords and ladies born on the height,
In being guests of ours, we who have toiled
Our upward way, and made the bread we eat
With sweat of our own brows.

Joan.   'Tis but a figure,
You'll understand, sweet ladies—though for meals
He might have found a better.

Lady F.   Nay, good dame,
No need to excuse; I love the honest ring
Of his rough rugged speech.

Joan.   Your ladyship
Thinks him so very rough? Yet let me say,
Honest and rough and rugged as he looks,
He's not an atom more so in his heart
Than the smoothest of them all.

Lady F.   O I doubt not.

Joan. He puts not all his varnish and deceit

On his outside, like that young coxcomb lord
Who sat in yonder place till yesterday—
More daintily trimmed up, and combed and curled,
And softer-spoken maybe——
  Sir Ruf.   Softer-spoken!
Such hard words as he cudgelled us withal
I never felt before. What of him now?
Know you if still he holds his lonely state
In the lodging left him by his father's care?
  John. Ay, as I think. A while ago I sent
One of my serving-men to ask if aught
There was he wished for and that I could give—
For, as you know, I bear him no ill-will——
  Lord F. O surely not.
  John.   Nay, rather pity him
With my whole heart.
  Sir Ruf.   As truly do we all.
  Lady F. O all.
  John.   But with harsh voice and rough
    he bade
My messenger begone.
  Joan.   Ay—with such airs
As I might give myself with one who came
To ask, not to bestow.
  Hub.   And since last night
Out of that crazy kennel he hath not stirred?
  John. E'en so.
  Amab.   For me, I always thought him
    strange.

Geral. As with the father so with the son, it seems.

Lord F. I marvel he could trust himself to sleep
In such a place—so damp and so unaired.

John. I know not if he slept; they say all night
His light was seen to burn.

Sir Ruf. Asleep or wake,
He will be damp enough if he but try
That hole a second night; hark to the rain,
Raining as though Heav'n fain would put out——

Lett. Nay!

Sir Ruf. The other place. Against such rain as this
Yon roof will serve no better than a sieve.

Hub. And the wind too! enough to crumple up
His hovel to the shape of a grape-skin squeezed.

Lord F. 'Tis a wild night indeed, and fit to chill him
To the bones with cold and damp. [*To a Servant.*] I pray you draw
That screen a little closer.

Sir Ruf. And by now
He must feel pinched for want of food and drink.
This way the flagon, please.

Lord F. I'll have more too;
This wine is excellent good. Ay, as you say,
He must be hard put to it, and in sooth
My heart is sore with pity.

John. Mine the same—

Though the fault is all his own if aught he lacks.
Another log, to keep the chill air out.
    Lord F. With perfect comfort and enjoyment, friend,
I fear you mean to spoil us.

                  Enter LILIAS.

    Hub.   Lo where comes
A dainty lass, to add to our good cheer.
Right welcome are you, fair one.
    Lili. [*To* JOHN.]   'Tis with you
I come to speak.
    Hub.   Will you not sit? here's room.
    Lord F. Our worthy host's relation, is't not so?
    John. A kind of a relation, sir, but poor—
Nay, very poor.
    Lord F.   Not an uncommon kind.
    Joan. One we had pity on, and have bred up
For sake of charity.
    Lord F.   That's a rarer sort.
    Sir Ruf. Rare! nay, a phenix. Sit you down, fair maid.
    Joan. You may, since you are asked, though you might sure
Be comelier apparelled for our feast.
    Lili. I came not for your feast, but to deliver
A prayer I'm charged with to my uncle John.
    John. And whose prayer may that be?
    Lili.   Poor old Tom Tod's.

Word hath been sent him on your part to-day
That he must give his little holding up
To his next neighbour, who doth covet it.

John.   And who besides can pay the rent thereof,
Which your Tom cannot.

Lili.   Yet if you but heard
How sore he pleads! If he must leave the home
That hath been his so long, he fain must house,
He and his daughter and his daughter's babes,
In the cold roofless fields, with the wind-pierced hedge
His warmest shelter.

John.   Can he pay his rent?

Lili.   Will you not see him? if you heard his tale
'Twould move you surely. Through the gath'ring storm
He hath journeyed all these miles, and now awaits
Your pleasure, so mishandled and tired out
With boist'rous buffets of the blust'ring wind
On his shrivelled grey outside, and with the pinch
Of inward sorrow, that to look at him
And grant his suit were one.

John.   Good reason then
For looking at him not. I have already
Made bargain with his neighbour. Honoured sirs,
You do not drink.

Joan.   I marvel how you dare
Disturb our entertainment of our guests
With such like toys and trash.

Lili.   Because a chance
Of doing good, or mending one's own wrong,

Is as a treasure, which by my neglect
I'd not have any lose. Will you not take?
'Tis offered still—but for how long who knows?
 John. You have my answer, and shall have none
  else.
Sit down and eat and drink, and plague no more.
 Lili. Your pardon; I'll go comfort as I may,
Yon poor old man—till better comfort comes.
[*Aside.*] Strange that so long it tarries. [*Exit.*
 John.   Not indeed,
I hope, your honours, that I cannot be
Soft-hearted with the best, but to do aught
Tending to foster 'mong the common sort
A spirit of indolence and servitude,
Of leaning upon others for their aid,
Is what we should be very careful of.
 Lord F. Just so, just so; too careful none can be.
 Sir Ruf. 'Tis what I always say.
 Lord F.   That delicate sense
Of rough, rude, sturdy, stubborn independence,
A sense so delicate and so eas'ly marred,
And yet the poor man's chiefest ornament——
O very careful.
 Sir Ruf. 'Tis like taking up
The butterfly to cherish and admire,
And rubbing off the bloom.
 Lord F.   There is a kind
Of selfishness about it.
 John.   So in truth

I am constrained to think—but my poor lord,
He heeded not these things, and, as I fear,
Hath done much harm that I must strive to cure.
    Lord F. He had no judgment.
    Sir Ruf.   No reflection.
    Hub.   None.
    Lady F. I cannot pardon folly like to his.
    Lord F. O greatly to be blamed.
    John.   I am afraid
He must be blamed—yet I feel for him much.
    Lord F. And I too; who would not? this is a
        case
Wherein the more one blames the more one feels.
    John. Ay, and the more one feels the more one
        blames;
'Tis even so.
    Lord F.   Precisely.
    John.   It appears
I ne'er can hope to see him in this life,
But you are present, sirs, to hear me say,
As without fear I may, that the one thing
To my contentment lacking is the face
Of my poor lost young lord.

                  Enter LIONEL.

    Lion.   And here it is,
To fill your measure of enjoyment full.
Why, how is this? you seem not so well pleased
As from your speech I hoped.

John. O yes, well pleased,
In faith exceeding pleased—but, I confess,
Ta'en something by surprise. And if you think
What words you laid upon us all last night,
You scarce can wonder that you find us now
For your return a little unprepared.
　Joan. Or I might even say much unprepared.
　Lord F. Truly 'tis very sudden.
　Lion. But I hope
Not quite unwelcome?
　John. O I would not say
Unwelcome—nay, not altogether so.
Be pleased to sit, and lay aside your cloak.
　Lord F. Indeed you had best; it must be damp,
　　I know.
　　[LIONEL *throws off his cloak, and sits down.*
　Lion. How shall I give my good friends thanks
　　enough
For kindness so o'erwhelming?
　John. Well, perchance
There are not many would be found so willing
To lend the hand of fellowship again
Where but last night it met with doubled fist.
You have hurt me in my feelings much, my lord,
And I must hope you'll bear in mind henceforth
I have a right to enjoyment of my own ;
And that for you to feel dislike thereof
Only because it chances what is now
Mine, once was yours, is not quite reasonable.

Lord F. You must see that yourself. Upon my word
'Tis excellently argued.

Lion. Not maybe
Quite reasonable, yet surely natural,
And to be pardoned.

John. Natural or not,
You cannot say that if I have your land,
It was not bought and paid for with hard gold;
You made the bargain, and must stand by it
As patiently as I.

Lion. A better bargain
Methinks for you than me.

John. O as for that,
It pleases you to say so—but, dear ladies,
Did you only know——Acres enough, I grant,
But so uncared for and so profitless,
Held by such pampered tenants——Witness all,
I would I had my good gold back again,
And he his land; that safely may I say.

Lion. 'Twere shame to keep you waiting for your
wish.

[*To a Servant.* Ho! friend, that bag I trusted to
your charge—
Bring here, and lay it on the board, in front
Of Master John of the Scales. [*The Servant places a
bag before* JOHN.] Now have you back
Your gold, and I my land; though, as I think,
Poor as your bargain was, you'd hold it fast
Were the four-and-twenty hours of grace run out;

But since they yet are not, why, yours is yours,
And mine is mine again.
John. What meaning's here
I cannot fathom.
Lion. You need only fathom
To the bottom of that bag; there will you find
My meaning clear enough.
John. [*Opening the bag.*] It looks like coin—
But cannot be, you know.
Joan. [*Rising, and coming round to* JOHN.] O,
 cannot be—
Against all reason. Bite them, ring them. What!
Good? You're a fool, and know not good from bad.
Give here. And if it chances this is good,
That proves not for the rest.
John. And who shall say
They are right counted either?
Lion. Count and weigh,
And bite and ring; no error shall you find.
[*To the others.*] How now, dear friends! I see
 amazement in you
Wrestles with joy which shall be uppermost;
Let it be joy, I pray, for know, the gold
That there you see is to the store behind
But as a little spilling on the road
From an o'erloaded wain. You thought me rich,
But all my riches were as poverty
To the wealth which for me had been from me hid,
And in safe keeping lay beneath the floor

N

Of the ruined hut that I in folly mocked.
 Lord F. Let me congratulate——
 Lion.   How well I knew
That I might count upon you all to hail
My strangely mended fortunes! And I see—
See by your faces blossoming into smiles,
And lips with friendship ready to o'erflow,
Like rivers in the sunshine of the spring—
That I mistook you not.
 Lord F.   Of that be sure;
So glad I never was.
 Sir Ruf.   In faith, nor I.
 Hub. Old friend, I give you joy.
 Lion.   No need to tell.
I read your hearts in the eyes of all of you,
And see that I require not e'en to excuse
My churlishness last night, since with your pardon
'Tis blotted out already.
 Lady F.   Nay, my lord,
There ne'er was aught to pardon.
 Lord F.   All my sorrow
Was that I could not for the moment lay
My hand on the little sum——
 Lion.   Think not of that.
 Hub. For me, remorse hath pricked me ever since
I was so quick to take offence for nought.
But, as you know, 'tis the highest-mettled horse
That's put the easiest out.
 Lion.   True, very true;

Who that knows aught of horses knows not this?

Sir Ruf. I lay awake pondering all the night
How I might let you have that loan, and think
I now have found a way, if you have still
The least occasion——

Lion. How am I to thank?
But now my need is past. O my kind friends,
Seek not to make excuse; I know how deep
It cut your faithful hearts to be constrained
Aught to deny me.

Lord F. That in truth it did.

Lion. And one is here whose pain must sure have
  been
Sharpest of all, since to her lot it fell
To deal the heaviest stroke. Fair Geraldine,
Was this not so? But O before you speak,
That struggling sigh, escaping with such force
From the white prison of your breast, betrays
What then you suffered and what then you hid.

Geral. I will not say, my lord, but that last night
It cost me much to speak the words I did;
Yet what could I choose else, being commanded
By father and by mother?

Lion. What indeed?
Sweet maid and pure—sweet as thrice-sugared milk,
And pure as the white froth thrown up by the sea,
The froth that Venus sprang from. And now, friends,
That I have looked to the bottom of your souls,
And stirred to the depths the filthy reeking slime

Of hidden putrefaction that doth make
Your surface shine so fair and iris-like,
Now have I done with you, and am content
That from my presence and my house you go
With all the speed you may.
    Lord F.   Here is some jest,
But one that I confess doth need for me
To be unriddled.
    Lion.   I'll unriddle straight.
Hence from my roof before your foulness breed
A pestilence in the air! How now! if speech
Hath lost its meaning for your ears, I'll find
Another way to deal. Here are my servants,
Who will obey me now I am rich again.
Good fellows, do you see that company
Of smell-feast lords and ladies, and that pair
Counting their money? Out with them forthwith
From my sight and from my doors. Haul them or
    push,
Or whip—I care not what—but out with them
This moment from my house.
    A Servant.   This moment, sir?
Alas! it rains just now so that well-nigh
It seems that one might swim from earth to heaven.
    Lion. Although this dwelling were the one firm
    point
In the black deep of space, they should not stay.
Hence with them, hence — or with my sword I'll
    help. [*Drawing.*

SCENE II.] *THE HEIR OF LINNE.* 175

 Lord F. No need, no need; we are going. [*To
  the others.*]   Pray you haste;
We shall be murdered else. Farewell, sweet lord;
Believe, we would not thwart you for the world.
 John. Not for the world, my lord. Methought I
  heard
A coin that rolled——but 'tis no matter—nay,
Not for the world.
 Joan.   Can you not make more speed?
 Lion. [*Seating himself as the rest go out.*] Farewell, friends all, farewell; I kiss your hands.
       [*Exeunt all except* LIONEL.
So, 'tis well done. Thus is the war declared,
The war that ne'er shall cease 'twixt me and men.
         [*The Scene closes.*

SCENE II.

A Corridor.

Enter LORD *and* LADY FITZWATER, HUBERT, *and*
 GERALDINE, *with Servants rolling along chests
 and bales.*

 Lady F. You are sure we take away all that we
  brought?
And the gifts too? no need to leave behind
Aught that is ours, whether it hath been ours
Long time or short.
 Geral.   I've ta'en all mine.

Hub.   And I.
Lord F. Hark to the wind; it howls about the house
As a wolf that hungers for us.

Enter SIR RUFUS ROLLESTONE, AMABEL, *and* LETTICE.

                                 And to think
That I must travel such a night as this!
A night indeed when one would almost need
Sailors for coachmen.
    Amab.   You are not, my lord,
The only one; we have to travel too,
We who gave not perchance so much offence
As some of you.
    Lett.   My feathers will be spoiled.
    Geral. I marvel any are of soul so tame
That they can wish to tarry in a house
Where insult hath been done them. As for me,
I long to shake its dust from off my feet.
    Sir Ruf. You'll not have far to go before the dust
Will be most thoroughly laid.

Enter another Servant.

    Ser.   My master sends
To know the reason of this tarrying.
    Lord F. You told him of the horror that I had
Of the rain-soaked air?
    Ser.   Ay.

Lord F.　　　　　　　　And he said?
Ser.　　　　　　　　　　　　　　He laughed.
Lord F. Laughed!
Ser.　　　　　　　And in very truth the dampest air
Were safer for you than his wrath to-night.
　　Lord F. I'm ready, friend. My coach waits?
　　Ser.　　　　　　　　　　　　　　　　Ay my lord;
[*To* SIR RUFUS.] And yours, sir, too.
　　Lord F.　　　　　　　　　　Pray help me with my cloak.

　　　　Enter JOHN *and* JOAN, *laden with packages.*

　　Ser. How now! you twain yet here! 'Twere best make haste,
Unless you'd have my lord come forth himself
To speed your parting.
　　John.　　　　　　We are going now;
Can you not see? Would you but deign, kind friends,
To lend us in the coach of one of you
A little, little room; or else must I,
I and my wife——
　　Joan.　　　　　　And his poor wife——
　　John.　　　　　　　　　　　　Go forth
Uncovered in the storm.
　　Lord F.　　　　　Are the shawls stowed?
　　Ser. Ay, and all else. This way.

John. Will you not, friends?

[*Exeunt all except* JOHN *and* JOAN.

Pursed-up-mouthed wretches!

Joan. Well, I hope you see
The fool you were ever to pay your court
To such as these. A scornful staring set,
Who if they sheltered in your house from a shower
Would bid you wipe your own chair ere they sat.

John. I pay my court to them! 'twas you, not I;
I held them in too much contempt.

Joan. I say
'Twas you, and you had best say otherwise.
For me, I scorned them always.

John. Let it be;
And think with me of what is now to do.

Joan. To foot it in the rain.

John. Ay, ay, but thus
We may come sooner to four walls and a roof
Than peradventure those proud-stomached ones,
For all their coaches—and high horses too.
We'll cross the little foot-bridge up the stream,
And of the farmer on the other side
Ask shelter for the night; he'll not deny
While we have this to show. [*Tapping his money-bag.*
What! cheer up, wife,
We've much to live for yet—indeed no less
Than five-and-twenty thousand golden crowns.

Joan. And that is true enough.

John.   A truth we hold,
A truth that nought can ever make us lose.

     Enter LILIAS.

What! girl! is't you? I had well-nigh forgot
That we must take you too. You come in time;
Help us with some of these.
 Lili.   Nay, I come not
To share your journey, but to bid farewell.
There is none now to whose bounty you can turn
To pay you what I cost, nor am I willing
To be on yours a burden.
 Joan.   'Tis a feeling
Finer than I had looked for. But yet come;
You've learned my ways, and of a serving-maid
I shall have need, I hope. Come then, nor fear
But I shall give you work.
 Lili.   Your pardon, nay—
Another service I will rather take,
And go forth on my way alone to seek.
And till I find it, why, this brooch, the gift
Of our kind lord, will keep me at least in bread.
 Joan. Well, saw you e'er unthankfulness like this?
A girl whose helplessness we fed and warmed
At our own hearth—or if not quite our own,
'Twas all the same—and now that she hath learned
To be of some slight use, she turns her back!
 John. Monstrous ingratitude! But the more I live,
The more I see the hollowness of the world.

Re-enter Servant.

Ser. What! loiter yet! Nay, then, I must fetch
whips.
John. No, no, we go, you see we go.
Ser. I see,
And still will see, until I see you out.
John. O vile, ungrateful, bad, base, wicked world!
[*Exeunt* JOHN *and* JOAN, *followed by Servant.*
Lili. And now must I go too, and lead my life
Far from this place and him. A dreary life,
As drear as blindness fall'n a second time
On one who once hath from afar beheld
The sunlight shining on the fields, and longed—
An autumn life, fed but on memories,
Save that with me summer hath never been.
What! can I murmur? I who see myself
Bless'd more than e'er in dreams I thought to be,
I who have been his rescuer from death,
And giv'n him back again to life and hope—
Is't not enough for me? What though no more
I look him in the eyes? So long he lives,
And in his life takes joy, so long he is mine—
Mine though he knows it not, and ne'er shall know.

Enter TOM TOD.

Tom. O me! what shall I do? what shall I do?
Lili. Friend Tom! How now! have you not
heard the news?

That our good lord has come to his own again,
And wrong shall be made right?
 Tom.   Come to his own!
Ay, but the devil first has come to him.
 Lili. Tom! What means this? I say our lord is
  back;
Find him, and all is well.
 Tom.   But I have found,
And all is ill.
 Lili.   You tell me you have asked
His leave to keep your farm, and been denied?
 Tom. 'Tis what I tell you, and 'tis what is true.
I'm lost and ruined, ruined and undone,
Like a stocking ravelled down from knee to toe—
And the poor children too, like little socks.
 Lili. Weep not, weep not; some error sure is here.
You saw him not yourself?
 Tom.   Ay, but I did.
They told me he had bid them keep me out,
But I would not believe, and past them pushed,
And down before him fell upon my knees.
 Lili. And he?
 Tom.   Looked up from leaning on his
  hand,
And bade me take my loathly face away—
He said, my loathly face.
 Lili.   How could he?
 Tom.   Yes,

I wondered too. And then he said, 'Begone
For an old hypocrite.'
  Lili.   But he knew not
The need that you were in?
  Tom.   'Tis true I scarce
Could speak for shaking, yet I told him all—
That my next neighbour had got leave to take
My farm, and if 'twere ta'en I must go starve;
But when I had done he only scowled, and said
He would not lift a little finger up
To keep from starving all that walked the earth
Upon two legs, so be they were not birds.
  Lili. He jested then.
  Tom.   Like jesting he looked not,
But cruel as I ne'er had seen him yet.
And after that, I thought my only chance
Would be to bring to his mind how I had once
Held him a baby in my arms, and kissed
His little cheek as soft as duckling's down.
And so I did—but he, he swore an oath,
And said that what I said made him ashamed
E'er to have been a baby. These indeed
Were his very words, and then I felt, as 'twere,
A kind of ball roll up and down my throat,
And could not answer aught, and came away.
  Lili. He that was once so good!
  Tom.   Can you not help?
And yet how can you? Nay, 'tis sure enough

I must go starve, and the sooner I begin
The sooner I shall finish.
  Lili.   Help! I help!
Help you! help him! O if I could! And yet—
Maybe——Tom, I will try. Get you again
To the fire, and warm you, and await my news.
I'll try.
  Tom. Heav'n bless and prosper you!
  Lili.   Amen.
                            [*Exeunt.*

SCENE III.

The Banqueting-room of Scene I.

LIONEL *discovered sitting as before.*

  Lion. Ay, there is still some pleasure in my life,
That life I must not part with, and am doomed
To wear till it rots from me; but I see
It hath some joys yet left—the joy at least
Of griping fast mine own, and with a 'No'
Baffling the arts of fawners and of liars.
I used to think 'twas only sweet to give;
But to deny to greed, to send away
Hypocrisy chop-fall'n, and flattery
With its crisp smirk damped out—to have the thing
That all men covet, and to hold it tight—
This is a pleasure of a daintier taste,
And one that uses not its own means up,

But, being indulged in, leaves the epicure
As able for indulgence as before.

Enter a Servant.

What would you? Am I never to have rest
From sight of a man's face?
   Ser.   I humbly crave
Your honour's pardon, but I come to know
What 'tis your honour's pleasure we should do
With the lords and ladies who were late your guests,
And who have sent to entreat——
   Lion.   Ha! they dare
     stay
When I have bid them go?
   Ser.   Nay, good my lord,
They went long since, but are come back again.
The river hath o'erflowed, and choked the roads,
So that with peril they were forced to turn
Their half-drowned coaches back, and now make
     prayer
For a night's shelter underneath your roof.
   Lion. And what are they that I should heed their
     prayer?
   Ser. They are very cold, my lord, and comfort-
     less,
And with no other cover from the storm
Than the coaches wherein dismally they sit.
   Lion. Let them still sit in their coaches, and be
     glad.

SCENE III.] *THE HEIR OF LINNE.*

Away, torment me not. Stay, yet a word—
The horses, if they will, they may undo,
And in the stables house; those beasts are dumb,
And have not learned from one another guile.
Stand not and stare, but go.

   Ser. [*Aside.*]   What change is here!
                                                      [*Exit.*

Enter another Servant.

   Lion. Another man!
   Ser.   'Tis not my fault, my lord.
I am sent by John and Joan of the Scales,
To implore you and beseech——
   Lion.   Am I defied
In mine own house? I bade you drive them forth,
And am I not yet rid of them?
   Ser.   Indeed
We did our best, my lord, and made them go;
But with them hath the storm played battledore,
And sent them back again.
   Lion.   Then let your whips
Play battledore upon the other side.
Out with them from my house.
   Ser.   Nay, in your house
Without your lordship's leave 'twas not for us
To let them come. They stand outside the gate,
But in such wet and shiv'ring plight that sure
You'd pity if you saw.
   Lion.   I pity! I!

Ser. They have been soused in the river, and there left
Whate'er they had—their bag of gold and all.
   Lion. Ha! how? Faith, that should be a pleasant tale.
   Ser. Crossing the crazy bridge that spans the stream
Just o'er the fall, their weight, it seems, quite finished
The work of wind and wave, and brought it down
Into the torrent, which had caught them too
But for a friendly tree whereat they clutched,
So that they passed not o'er the perilous edge,
And through the water struggled back to land.
   Lion. For the water a fair riddance. But the gold?
   Ser. 'Scaped from them as they fell, and leapt the torrent
Into the stream below.
   Lion.   Here's what will make
That stream worth angling in.
   Ser.   Alas! my lord,
You know they say the torrent at that place
Hath bored a hole to the middle of the earth,
And ne'er was seen again what there was lost.
   Lion. So have I heard indeed. And now begone;
I've had enough.
   Ser.   We have your leave, my lord,
To lodge them for the night?
   Lion.   Do I seem one

So babyish of resolve, that what I once
Have as my will laid down I can be tickled
With grins and bows to swerve from? I said No,
And No I say again.

Ser. For me, there's much
I've had to bear from John and Joan too;
But now to see them stand and wring their hands,
So humbly and so drippingly—in sooth,
I cannot choose but pity.

Lion. Hence, thou slave,
I'll not be schooled by thee, thou whose mere presence,
Being a man's, offends me. Leave my sight,
Or thou shalt fare the worse.

[*Exit Servant.*

I know that fellow
Doth deem me cruel. Cruel! Once, to read
Of cruel men and deeds raised in my heart
A loathing like to pain; now I believe
The cruel men of the world have been the best,
Who have found the others out. Call they me cruel?
'Tis they are cruel—they, who, though they see
That I am fain to shun them like the plague,
Will leave me yet no peace. O how to 'scape
Where I shall be alone, with no man's face,
Or voice, to put me e'er in mind again
Of the thing that once I was! I'll build myself
A dungeon underground, where I will hide
In darkness with my gold, too deep to hear
The noise of the world above. Nay, better still,

I'll have a hill-top fort, hedged round with guns,
Which none may venture near, but all may see,
And each to other say, 'There dwells the man
Who hath gold and will not give;' this were in one
Safety and sweet revenge.

> LILIAS, *who, in her white veil, has entered unperceived a few moments before, glides from behind a screen.*

Lili. Who is't that speaks
Of the sweetness of revenge?

Lion. Thou dost vouchsafe
Once more thy presence?

Lili. Ay, for the last time.
Nor hadst thou seen me now but for thy faults,
Which have disturbed my peace. O then heed well
The last words thou shalt ever hear me speak.

Lion. The last! And why the last?

Lili. Ask not,
but hear.
I come to chide thee.

Lion. What is my offence?
Thou, that canst read my heart, see'st there no thought
Of thee, that is not rev'rent and submiss.

Lili. Yet did I bid thee of thy second wealth
Make wiser use than of thy first; but worse,
Thousandfold worse, not better, dost thou deal
With it and with thyself.

Lion. What have I done?

Lili. Denied thy justice to the innocent,
Thy mercy to the weak, set in the place
Of trust unreasoning more unreasoning hate,
Closed up thy purse and heart 'gainst man and Heaven.

Lion. I was deceived before by knaves and liars,
And will not be again.

Lili. 　　　　　Who makes amends
For an old fault by that fault's opposite
Doth but commit new fault. No knaves and liars
Deceived thee yet so much, thou heir of Linne,
As thou deceiv'st thyself, in thinking now
That knaves and liars make up all the world.

Lion. I have found none else in it.

Lili. 　　　　　　　　Because thou ne'er
Hast ta'en the way to find. Believe me well,
The world unto each man is what each man
Hath made it for himself, and thou mad'st thine
With neither choice nor care, so that the worst,
Seeing thy wealth and weak unguarded state,
Were brought about thee as about a prey,
While the best shunned thee, scorning to be thought
Base as the others, or with them to herd.

Lion. Some good is then in men?

Lili. 　　　　　　　　As thou shalt find
When thou shalt rightly seek—with courtesy,
Wise bounteousness, and large good-will to all

Winning the worthiest, yet with wakeful eye
Ne'er lulled asleep by buzz of flattery
Making the unworthy fear thee as a judge.
Thus live henceforward, meeting other men
Lovingly, yet not blindly, with a mind
Informed of worst and best; and though sometimes
Thou still may'st be deceived, yet oftenest
Thou shalt have cause to say the world is good—
Yea, e'en its evil shall but help thee more
To understand its worth, as by the dust
We see the path of the sunbeam in the air.

Lion. Since thou hast said it, I believe, and joy
That I can so believe, but send me not
To live 'mong men again; I'll be content
Out of my solitude to wish them well,
But more I cannot.

Lili. Why?

Lion. I have no skill
In them and in their ways. What! all my life
I've lived with them and sought to make them friends,
And yet in all my life, by man nor woman,
I never have been loved for mine own self.

Lili. If this so troubles thee, ne'er to have been loved,
Let it not vex thee more. Thou hast been loved,
No man more faithfully; so may'st thou hope
As one hath loved thee that another may—
As dearly, and more happily.

Lion. O say—
That one—who? who?
    Lili. This while on earth thou livest
Thou ne'er shalt know, but one who for thy sake
Would have been glad to lay down life and all.
If this may comfort thee, believe it true,
For true it is, though more thou may'st not know.
Wilt thou obey me now?
    Lion. O in all things!
All that thy sweet voice counsels will I do—
Go forth 'mong men, and with them live at peace,
Lay thoughts of vengeance down, and strive to pardon
Who most have wronged me; ay, e'en John of the Scales
Shall feel to-night in his heart some of that comfort
Which thou hast poured in mine.
    Lili. Wilt ever be
At one or other of two opposing poles?
John of the Scales no comfort needs from thee,
Being made rich with gains gained at thy cost.
Be bountiful, but let thy bounty flow,
If not on those that merit, yet at least
On those that need, and he you name needs nought.
    Lion. Say'st thou needs nought? Ha! then, another lie
They put upon me when they brought me word
His gold was lost in the river?

Lili.   His gold lost
In the river! what means this?
   Lion.   Thou ask of me!
Thou that shouldst know all things by power divine!
O dost thou mock me, or——   [*Pauses.*
   Lili.   What it imports
To know I know indeed.   How darest thou
So strangely look on me?
   Lion.   Yet didst thou ask,
And seem to stand amazed.   O art thou then
Subject to ignorance and wonderment—
And mortal like myself?
   Lili.   No further seek.
My time is come; farewell; remember her
Whom no more shalt thou see.
   Lion. [*Throwing himself in her way.*] I charge
      thee stay—
Or vanish if thou wilt; but o'er yon threshold
Thou shalt not pass till thou hast let me look
Upon thy face unveiled.
   Lili.   Make way, make way!
   Lion. Thy bosom heaves.   Can spirits be so
      moved
By mortal boldness?   I'll be bolder yet,
And touch thee—nay, I will.   [*Seizing her hand.*
                     Of flesh and blood
Warm like mine own.   What! think not now to
      'scape;
I have thee fast; unveil.

Lili.   O ask me not!
Forgive, forgive. I never did you hurt.
   Lion. Say rather thou hast loaded me with good—
Saved me from death, and sin. O canst thou deem
That I would harm thee, that thou tremblest thus?
   Lili. I fear not to be harmed. Strike if you will,
So you but let me go and seek no more.
   Lion. Not till I see thy face. Wilt thou not
      show?
Nay then, I must myself find how to unwind.
O tremble not, thou sweet-voiced and white-armed;
I'd rather give the life that thou hast saved
To a thousand deaths than hurt a hair of thine—
But look I must. O who? not Geraldine;
I am mad to think it.   [*Draws away her veil.*
            Lilias! [*She hides her face in
                          her hands.*
               And was't thou,
Thou from the first?
   Lili.   Because I could not bear
To see you wronged—and knew no other way
To give you warning. Pardon.
   Lion.   And thou too
That cam'st 'twixt me and death?
   Lili.   You once had
      hearkened;
I hoped you might again. O but I shame——
Beseech you, stay me not.
   Lion.   And this time comest

To save me from the darkest death of all,
The death whereto my soul had doomed my soul.

Lili. You see what fraud I put upon you. Now Forgive, and set me free.

Lion. Thou hadst for me
Such care, thou who seemedst ever chiefly bent
To find a way to shun me?—Can it be?
Lilias, thou saidst I had been loved. By whom?
By thee? Nay, speak—by thee?

Lili. O let me go—
I pray you, pray you. O be merciful.

Lion. Thou still wouldst go? But I would have
    thee stay—
To counsel me, and lead my steps aright,
So that they ne'er shall stray, to be my friend,
My guide, my northern star, my outer conscience,
Wherein, as in a mirror, I may read
If I do well or ill, my guardian saint,
And yet withal my cherished fostered wife.
This, Lilias, wilt thou be?

Lili. I am not worthy——
O that I might but go!

Lion. And go thou shalt
If with thy clear eyes looking into mine
Thy lips can tell me that thou ne'er hast loved.
Well, well? the answer? None? and trembling
    still?
Why then, my wife—my fast-betrothèd wife.

              [*Drawing her to his bosom.*

O take my thanks, kind Heaven, that at last
I know what love can be.
    Lili.   And mine with his.
    Lion. But now to show that I have learned the lesson
That thou and Heav'n have taught; yet could I wish
The task were heavier, for I find by proof
How easy 'tis for the happy to forgive.
What ho! my servants, ho!

            Enter a Servant.

                Throw open wide
My gates and doors, and let all enter in
Who wait for shelter; tell them on my part
I make them welcome to my roof to-night,
And food and fire, and all things else they need,
In honour of a new great happiness
That just hath come to me.   [*Exit Servant.*
              O now I feel
To thee my love went forth, or sought to go,
From the beginning, even from that day
I saw thee first—as fair and fresh and pure
As the new sweet breath of morning air that blows
Through the earliest opened casement. But indeed
Thou mad'st me think I only cumbered thee
By coming in thy sight.

Lili.　　　　　　　I was so poor,
So helpless to repay.
　　Lion.　　　　　And thus it chanced
My new-born love, still too untaught and young
To know itself, went wand'ring houseless forth,
And the first offered shelter blindly thought
To be its native home—how far wherein
Mista'en it now hath found, now from long travel
Returned unto its birthplace, there to dwell
Changeless, except in growth, for evermore.
　　Lili. What have I done that Heaven gives so
　　　　much?
　　Lion. O see where come my guests—nay, our
　　　　guests now.

Enter LORD *and* LADY FITZWATER, HUBERT, GERAL-
　　DINE, SIR RUFUS ROLLESTONE, AMABEL, LETTICE,
　　and all the other Guests, also JOHN *and* JOAN (*the
　　two last covered with mud*), TOM TOD *following*.

Friends (for I still will call you friends to-night,
Being still guests), you all are welcome back,
And shall be welcome still, until such time
As the skies give you leave to seek in peace
Your sev'ral homes—such of you as have homes;
The others [*Looking at* JOHN *and* JOAN] must I try to
　　　　fit with homes,
Since none of you I longer would detain
Than is most strictly needful.

Lord F. How to thank
Such kind, such gen'rous hospitality!
   Sir Ruf. We are much bound to your lordship's
      courtesy. [*Aside to* LORD FITZWATER.
      Although perchance a little dryly given.
   Lord F. Dryness is all I ask for. [*To* JOHN.] Pray
      you, friend,
A trifle further back; you are very damp.
   John. My dear young lord! Receive the thanks
      of one
Who has lost his little all.
   Joan. And his poor wife's.
   Lion. Make not your thanks to me, for here doth
      stand
Your benefactor of to-night, and mine;
To whom is due all good that in me is,
Or from me e'er shall come, and all the joy
Wherewith my soul abounds—already queen
Of my house and me, to-morrow my fair bride.
   Lady F. His bride! Who would have thought——
   Amab. [*To* LETTICE.] Poor Geraldine!
   Lord F. How pleasant is this fire! With all my
      heart
I give your lordship joy.
   Tom. O might I live
To kiss on the cheek a little lord again!
   John. His bride! But why, as well as I can see
For mud in my eyes, 'tis Lilias, my niece!

Lion.   Ay, Lilias your niece, who as my wife
Shall from to-morrow her sweet reign begin,
Though now her name is but — White Maid of
   Linne.

[*The Curtain falls.*

THE END.

TASSO.

PERSONS REPRESENTED.

ALFONSO, *Duke of Ferrara.*
SCIPIO GONZAGA, *of the Ducal house of Mantua, afterwards Cardinal.*
TORQUATO TASSO.
ASCANIO, *an old Courtier.*
FRANCESCO,
MADDALO, } *two other Courtiers.*
ANTONIO COSTANTINI, *a Friend of Tasso.*
FABRIZIO, *a Merchant of Mantua.*
GREGORIO, *his Friend.*
LORENZO, *betrothed, afterwards married, to Claudia.*
The Chamberlain of the Pope.
The Prior of the Monastery of St. Onofrio at Rome.
An Officer of the Pope.
A Physician.
A Warder of the Hospital of St. Anna at Ferrara.
A Page.

LEONORA, *Sister to the Duke.*
LIVIA,
ANGELICA, } *Ladies attending on Leonora.*

LAURA, *Daughter to Fabrizio.*
PETRONILLA, *Aunt to Laura.*
CLAUDIA, *Cousin to Laura.*

The Cardinal of Este and his train, the Papal Nuncio to Ferrara and his train, Courtiers of the Duke, Ladies of Leonora, Friends and Guests of Fabrizio, Roman Citizens, Monks, Attendants, &c.

The Scene of the First Act is laid at Mantua, of the Second, Third, and Fourth, in and near Ferrara, and of the Fifth, at Rome.

An interval of some years is supposed to pass between the First and Second Acts, also between the Third and Fourth.

TASSO.

ACT I.

SCENE I.

Mantua. The Garden of FABRIZIO'S *Villa.*

A party of young people discovered dancing, among them LORENZO *and* CLAUDIA. *LAURA sits playing to them on a lute. When the dance is ended, the partners distribute themselves in pairs over the stage, some walking about, others coming up to* LAURA.

Loren. [*Who comes up arm-in-arm with* CLAUDIA.
    Kind mistress Laura, take the thanks of all
For your sweet music.
    Clau.   I would thank her too,
But have not pardoned her. What! to sit still
Upon her birthday—to be queen of the feast,
And not to dance!—for shame!
    Loren.   And so say I,
And so say all.

Several.   Ay, all.
Lau.   Friends, cousin, nay;
If I am queen of the feast, it is my part
To minister to my guests, and this I do.
    Clau. But would do better if you led the dance.
Come, mend your manners now; 'tis not too late.
I'll be musician.   [*Trying to take* LAURA'S *lute.*
    Lau.   Pray you, cousin, no.
I am not in the mood to dance to-day.
    Clau. Not in the mood! here's logic!
    Lau.   And the lute
Is out of tune; heard you not how it jarred?
    Clau. What! the lute too not in the mood to-day!
    Lau. Give me a little time to try the strings,
And then we'll see. Nay, but beseech you, friends,
Wait not on me; go wander at your will
The garden through, and whatsoever flowers
You deem the fairest, cull them for your own;
I know to-day my father makes you welcome
To the choicest of his store. So for a while
Farewell; anon you shall be summoned back
For a new dance. [*Exeunt all except* LAURA, LORENZO,
    and CLAUDIA, *though some couples are seen passing
    up and down at intervals at the back part of the stage.*
    Clau.   Lorenzo, heard you not?
She bade you go.
    Loren.   Nay, not more me than you;
I stay because you stay.
    Clau.   That reason's none.

I am her cousin, with a cousin's rights.
  Loren. But you have giv'n your word to make me
    soon
Her cousin too. Nay, frown not, Claudia, love;
Have sweethearts then no rights?
  Clau.   Some have perchance.
Am I your sweetheart?
  Loren.   Ay.
  Clau.   Then have I right
To lay command on you for what I please;
And my command is, Go.
  Lau.   Nay, on my faith—
Cousin, you are too hard. Why should he go?
  Clau. To give me time to find the string that jars.
Obey, Lorenzo.
  Loren.   I see well I must.   [*Exit*
  Lau. Thou foolish cousin!
  Clau.   Not so foolish yet.
Laura, I know why you are out of tune,
And your lute not in the mood.
  Lau.   And say then why
  Clau. Because the student lean and pale from
    Padua,
Your poet-lover, is not here to-day.
  Lau. You mean the Signor Tasso?
  Clau.   Will nought serve
But you must hear his name? Well then, I'll say
The Signor Tasso—ay, to please you more,
Signor Torquato Tasso. I had thought

Your father gave consent he should be asked
To this your birthday feast, but your quenched looks
Tell me it is not so.

Lau.   Now see how ill
You read my looks! He is asked, and he will come—
Will come—hath promised.

Clau.   But is not come yet?

Lau. We know not how he is busied; he hath things
Higher than others have to engross his thoughts.

Clau. What should be higher in a lover's count
Than leave to approach his mistress? Cousin, cousin,
I wish you ne'er had seen him.

Lau.   Then you wish
As I wish not. And wherefore wish you so?

Clau. Because I hold all poets in distrust.
I am not used to poets.

Lau.   That is sure.
But I, who know them better—taught by him—
Deem that a man with nobler, fairer thoughts
Than other men should be of greater faith,
Not less, than they.

Clau.   Should be—that's true.

Lau.   You think
He hath forgot my birthday—but not so.
Here is the proof—this paper, sent this morn.
                [*Drawing a paper from her bosom.*

[*Reading.*] *With leaves of that bright tree of fame*
           Whereof she shares the glorious name—
Laura and laurel—a conceit he loves—

    Ye nymphs, crown Laura's brow to-day.
    Or with the flowers, whereof no less
    She shares the blushing loveliness——
Nay, there he flatters, and I'll read no more;
But 'twas a fault he made for love of me.
     [*Kissing the paper as she puts it back.*
 Clau. Ay, so far gone? Well, if I may not wish
You ne'er had seen him, I may wish at least
He were no poet.
 Lau.   'Tis as though you wished
That he were not himself.
 Clau.   Yet must you own
Your loves had prospered better were he none.
Would he have only pinned his soaring thoughts
Down to the study of the law, whereof
He was a follower when you knew him first,
Your father by this time had let you wed,
Who now forbids you e'en to be betrothed
Until he hath some better proof than now
That one who is a poet to his trade
Is not by trade a beggar. Is it wrong
To wish your poet were a lawyer still?
 Lau. Ay, when you know the law was unto him
So sore a yoke it made him by its weight
A burden to himself.
 Clau.   Yet have I heard
Love makes all burdens light.
 Lau.   Cousin, no more.
He chose well, choosing not to drag the chain

Of a calling that he loathed; and even thus
Would I have had him choose. He told me once
That I was born to give his spirit wings;
And shall I now be found a sordid clog
To bind him down to muddy cares of earth,
And soil those wings, and lame their glorious flight?

 Clau. I'm glad that my Lorenzo has no wings.
Hush, hush—your father.

   Enter FABRIZIO, GREGORIO, PETRONILLA, *and
     others.*

 Fab.   Ay, friends, I believe
The house is in good taste—and garden too;
To builder and to gardener both I gave
Strict orders for good taste.

 Pet.   And well they knew
My brother was a man who ne'er failed yet
To pay for what he ordered.

 Fab.   That, indeed,
I hope all know of me. I'm a plain man,
An honest, simple burgher, and no more,
But always paid my way. I'll make a note
To have those roses cropped; their straggling spoils
The smoothness of the hedge.

 Pet.   Why, how now, girls!
What do you here alone? I fear, niece Laura,
You make but a slack hostess.

 Fab.   'Tis her fault

To be always shy. 'Tis well I find you, child,
For, as I think, 'tis time we asked our guests
To come and make some trial of what repast
May wait for them within.
 Lau.   We had thought first
To have one other dance.
 Fab.   One other dance!
Always one other dance with you young folks!
 Greg. 'Tis even so—while we poor old ones wait.
The young are very selfish, and 'tis fit
Selfishness should be curbed.
 Fab.   Let's in.
 Lau.   But, father,
Are all our guests yet come?
 Fab.   Ay, all methinks—
Nay, not indeed the Signor Tasso yet,
But for his fault we others need not starve.
 Pet. [*Aside to* FABRIZIO.] The Signor Tasso,
  brother! was it well
He should be asked to-day?
 Fab. [*Aside to* PETRONILLA.] Had he not been,
She would have deemed me tyrant and him saint,
And as a saint he would have wrought more wonders
Absent than present. If I shut my clerks
In the back room at fair-time they will do
No work at all for thinking of the show;
If in the front, they look, and, having looked,
Turn back unto their books. [*Aloud.*] Go some of
  you

And call our guests together; 'tis full time
We were at table, let who will be late.

Greg. There's the right spirit, friend Fabrizio.
For me, I would not have my cook put out
Though 'twere to wait for the duke's self—much less
A trencher-scraping student. For I think
This Tasso that you speak of is the same
Who went to Padua to study law,
But took to writing verses?

Fab. Ay, the same—
Would I could say he were a wiser man.

Greg. A beggarly poor choice—so beggarly
I should have judged him likelier to come
Betimes to your good fare than keep himself—
And others—fasting.

Clau. [*Aside to* LAURA, *who makes a movement of
impatience.*] Nay, he is but surly
Because he has not dined.

Pet. [*Aside.*] Is't thus he speaks
Of guest of ours? [*Aloud.*] Neighbour Gregorio,
This Signor Tasso, though, I grant you, poor—
And poor enough—yet springs of noble blood,
And here in Mantua are none so great
But make him welcome; yea, his closest friend
Is the duke's own kinsman, Signor Scipio.

Greg. He who was sent to study for the church?

Pet. Ay, even he; the twain are rather brothers
Than fellow-students.

Greg. Prince and churchman! here

Was patronage for a lawyer! And he chose
Rather to be a poet—I would say
A fool, but 'tis all one.
    Pet.   Ay, fool indeed.
I take his part no further than to avouch
He is fit company for whom you will;
But when you say a fool, so say I too.
    Lau. And yet, perchance——[*Pauses.*
    Pet.   What! Laura, did you speak?
    Lau. Perchance, Aunt Petronilla, 'twas because
He chose the poet's, not the lawyer's, part
That such high friendship as you speak of now
Is his at all.
    Pet.   What mean you? And is't you
Whose fault is to be shy?
    Lau.   I mean, 'tis like
His Excellence the Signor Scipio,
Seeing in him what noble minds most prize,
A nobler than himself——
    Pet.   A nobler! What!
He nobler than the Signor Scipio!
Child, are you mad?
    Greg.   A poor starved paper-spoiler
More noble than the kinsman of the duke!
She says it for a jest.
    Lau.   No, for the truth.
If this Torquato Tasso be indeed
The poet he is held by those most skilled,
He may claim kin more high than any duke.

A poet is a prophet sent by Heaven
From time to time on earth, to show to men
Heav'n's type of beauty and of nobleness,
Whereof the God-giv'n sense, not being thus
New-grafted in their hearts, would perish soon
Of the grossness of the soil. This nobleness,
This beauty, all the greatest ones of earth
Make their chief task to copy as they can
In deeds of arms, in pageantry of courts;
But while no more than imitators they,
The poet hath—nay, is—the thing itself.

Enter TASSO, *appearing from behind a hedge. He pauses for a moment, gazing at* LAURA, *then advances.*

   Tas. Fair mistress Laura.
   Lau.   [*Starting.*] You!
   Tas.   Yea, even I,
Who pray you for a birthday gift to take
These flowers, [*Giving her flowers.*] which, born of earth, may yet lay claim
To kinship with the skies. [*Aside to her.*] Laura, I heard,
And thought I heard the heav'nly muse herself
To whom my spirit is vowed. Be thanked, be thanked.
[*Aloud.*] Signor Fabrizio, I greet you well.
I fear I seem too tardy.
   Fab.   No excuse;
You are come, and shall be welcome.

Tas.   Could I think
That from so fair a company as this
My presence had been missed, the grudge I owe
To the cause that stayed me would be deeper yet.
But this I dare not either fear or hope.
   Greg. In sooth but you were missed, sir, and
      missed much—
And talked of by us all, as though nought else
Were worth the talking of.
   Tas.   Talked of by all!
Alack! how many faults must have been hit!
   Greg. Why, how should you know that?
   Tas.   Because I know
How foolish, blind, and ignorant of the world
And of themselves, all are behind their backs.
   Fab. Come, come, since you are here at last, 'tis
      time
We go within, and see what waits for us.
Are all assembled? [*Looking round at his guests, who are now all present, the dancers having gradually returned.*] Ay, 'tis so. In, friends;
And it may be that you will find the cook
Hath not forgot you quite.
   Tas. [*To* LAURA, *leading her apart from the others.*
                Stay here with me;
I have a word to say.
   Lau.   What should this be?
   Tas. News for your private ear.
   Fab.   Will none go first?

Nay, then, I'll lead the way.
    [*Exeunt all but* TASSO *and* LAURA.
Lau.   Well, sir, your news?
That you come late unto my birthday feast—
So late I thought you would not come at all?
    Tas. Nay, when you know the cause you will forgive.
Great fortune hath befall'n me.
    Lau.   Ay? O then
Befall'n me too. But how? Tell all—tell quick.
I knew that Heav'n would make us glad one day.
    Tas. You have sometimes thought I set my hopes
        too much
On great ones and their favour, but hear now
What they have wrought for me. The Cardinal
Of Este, brother to Ferrara's duke,
Being to Ferrara now upon his way
To greet his friends, will take me in his train,
And so commend me to the duke his brother
That at his court I both shall find a home
And special grace, as one whose praise or blame
Can vivify or wither through all time
The name it breathes on. Well, is this not news?
    Lau. That you should go in train of the Cardina
Unto Ferrara? was it thus you said?
    Tas. E'en so—Ferrara—golden home of art,
Foremost of courts, where a wise prince doth rule,
Who keeps the brightest glory of his smiles
For what can best reflect their glory back.

Lau. Ferrara! Then you will leave Mantua—
Leave Mantua—and me.
 Tas.   Sweet, for a time
It must be so indeed. How now! you weep?
Nay, nay, not thus, my Laura—pray thee nay;
Each tear of thine drops anguish in my heart,
So that thy sorrow is more sorrowful
To me than thee. Then let my kisses plant
New roses on thy cheek, and weep no more;
To weep thou hast no cause. Shall not my love
Be ever present to thee, and so serve
To keep me present too?
 Lau.   Then you will stay?
You will not go?
 Tas. How mean you?
 Lau.   And to please
My father's humour, you will turn again
To your old calling? not to give yourself
Wholly thereto, but so that he may see
You need no help from princes? And methinks
The work, albeit you love it not, would make
Your hours of leisure and of poesy
Seem sweeter-tasted. Yea, it shall be so;
Shall it not be, Torquato? for my sake?
 Tas. You said you loved me.
 Lau.   Ay, and said the truth.
 Tas. The truth! Yet now that of my hopes and
   toils
The glorious fruit hath ripened, and but waits

My outstretched hand to pluck it, now that Fame
Doth hold the golden cup, charged with the draught
That all men thirst for, to my parching lips—
Yea, makes herself a servant at my beck—
You step between, and bid me give up all
To be a hireling drudge. 'Twas needful much
To say you loved me, for I else had deemed
Such counsel was the counsel of a foe.

 Lau. Torquato!

 Tas.   Was it so? for foes I have—
I know it, though they go in guise of friends—
Who with their envy fain would hold me down;
But shall not; nay, not though unto their side
They have won thee too. [*She lays her hand on his
  arm.*] How is 't?

 Lau.   No more; forgive—
Though what I spoke amiss 'twas my love spoke,
And not the hate of others. But forgive;
Go to Ferrara, go where fortune calls,
And knowing what high fate awaits thee there
I'll strive to be as happy in thy going
As in thy staying I had found myself
Without the need of striving.

 Tas.   Why, there spoke
The Laura of my soul.

 Lau.   But promise me,
Promise that I shall be thy Laura still.

 Tas. What! since I am a wand'rer dost thou think
My love shall wander too? Not so, not so;

Swallows may come and go, and I with them,
But not my love of thee, which in my heart
Hath made its nest for ever.
 Lau.   Yet I fear
That the great ladies whom you there will find,
With their high-born cold-glitt'ring words and ways,
Will make me in your memory seem a thing
Still simpler than I am. Do you remember
That fancy that you told me of one day
For your great poem?—of a sorceress
Who by her beauty and her wiles had lured
A Christian champion to forget his faith
And duty for her sake? how by her art
She made a garden for his prison-house,
So fair, it seemed the art of Nature's self;
Where all the trees were gay with green and gold
Of bud and fruit at once, while through the leaves
Light-murmuring breezes and soft-throated birds
Trilled changeful music — and where white-limbed
  nymphs
Played to and fro, and smiled and blushed, and made
Their smiling by their blushes lovelier seem,
And by their smiles their blushing. And in midst
Of all this beauty, at the enchantress' feet,
Glorying in bondage as in conquest she,
The Christian knight lay prone, and fed his eyes
On false Armida's face. Did you not say
Her name should be Armida?
 Tas.   Ay. How well

Hast thou remembered, love! and O how fair
My fancies seem, when kissed by thy sweet lips!

Lau. Pray you, by no Armida e'er be wiled
Into forgetting me.

Tas.   O have no fear;
Thine image is my talisman. And e'en
Without it were I safe, being vowed to Fame,
And so made proof against an earthly lure.

Lau. Unless——

Tas.   Say on.

Lau.   Unless that Fame herself
Should be the false Armida of your life.
Indeed I cannot think Fame worth so much—
Being neither peace, nor yet true happiness—
That in her quest all else should be passed by.

Tas. Then have you never thought of what Fame
    is—
The birthright of great minds, in other minds
To live eternal life; and for this due
Of noble natures noble natures crave
As other men for bread, because the food
By Fate and Heav'n ordained them, and where most
The hunger, most the right. You love me, Laura,
Yet feel not this?

Lau.   But I will strive to feel
In all things e'en as you.

Tas.   And 'twill be well.
Else might I fear you were that sorceress,
The Armida that you warn me of, who fain

Would keep me in a flowery durance curbed
From that high office that I hold from Heaven.
 Lau. Armida! Not, I pray, that name for me
 Tas. So high an office and so glorious
That he who wields it is in right thereof
Made greater than the greatest ones of earth—
As you yourself late said, though now, it seems,
You grudge me such exalted fellowship.
 Lau. O deem not thus. I do but grudge perchance
To think that you should stoop to pay them court
And wait upon their favour.
 Tas. This I do
Because their worldly greatness is the staff
Whereon I have to lean to climb the heights,
Loftier than theirs, that are my proper home.
But lo, where comes of my great friends the best,
And in my love the greatest of them all.
 Lau. The Signor Scipio?
 Tas. Ay, even he.

Enter SCIPIO GONZAGA.

In happy time, kind friend. See, this is one
Of whom you oft have heard from me.
 Sci. How now!
The Laura upon whose triumphal name
You love to play in sonnets, crowning it
With leaves from its own tree? Fair lady, take
My double homage, both for you and him,

For, on my word, not Petrarch's laurels twine
More close round Petrarch's Laura than round you ,
The laurels of my friend.
 Lau.   To make my thanks
To your Excellence aright I know not how,
And can but say, you are welcome.
 Sci.   I must fear
I half shall spoil my welcome when I tell
What errand brings me. Friend, the Cardinal
Greets you, and warns you he hath now begun
His journey, and anon will pass these gates,
Where he will halt until you join his train.
So see that you be ready.
 Lau.   What! so soon!
You told me not it was to be so soon.
 Tas. It must be, love. Nay, nay, look not so sad;
Till our next meeting we will live on hope,
And, when we meet, on joy. [*To* Scipio.] Pray, of
  your friendship
One other service—unto those within,
Her father and his friends, to tell this news.
They know not yet; and from illustrious lips
My fortune will the more illustrious sound.
 Sci. I'll do your wish. Lady, be comforted;
He goes forth now, but to your arms one day
He shall be brought back famous, hailed by all
Italy's poet of poets. [*Exit into the house.*
 Tas.   Heard you that?

And it is true. Nature hath signed the bond
And giv'n it me to keep. Will not that day
Pay for the pain of this?
   Lau.   Indeed to see
Such day would make me prouder to be yours
Than you of being you.
   Tas.   And who shall say
But more than he hath promised thou shalt see?
Perchance—who knows?—perchance a visible crown
Of thine own leaves, thy laurels, on my head.
It is my dream, and sometimes dreams come true—
That even as that Petrarch, whose great name
We heard but now, was solemnly in Rome
Crowned with the poet's crown of living green,
And outward homage by all men performed
Unto his inward kingship, so shall I
One day in Rome wear crown.
   Lau.   And e'en as well
'Twould fit thy brow as his, or as the best
That e'er bore badge of greatness.
   Tas.   I shame not
To tell thee of the fancy, since the crown
I covet is not made of gold or gems,
But of green leaves unstained by blood or tears,
And therefore sure should bring more true content
Than crowns of kings—such true and full content
As I can never know until the day
That first it binds my brow.

Lau.   O when 'tis there,
Heav'n send that I may be where with mine eyes
I may drink in thy glory, though the sight
Were the last they e'er should see.
   Tas.   And when 'tis there,
Be sure 'twill be the dearer to my heart
For coming from thy tree, mine own sweet love,
My Laura and my laurel.
   Lau.   Nay, but look—
My father.

Enter, from the house, FABRIZIO, GREGORIO, PETRON-
   ILLA, LORENZO, CLAUDIA, *and the other guests,
   with* SCIPIO.

   Fab.   I am glad we come in time
To claim a little part in your farewells,
Which, as I see, already you begin.
   Tas. My friend hath told you, then?
   Fab.   Ay—and to say
Farewell, and of your fortune bid you joy,
We interrupt our feast.
   Greg.   That can I vouch—
In middle of the pasty.
   Tas.   I am bound
Unto your friendship much.
   Fab.   Why, as for that,
'Tis not because you travel by a road
That I love not, that I should therefore grudge

Good wishes for the journey.
Tas.   Yet I hoped
You would have seen by now that I had chosen
My road aright.
    Fab.   And so, maybe, I should,
But am too poor and plain a man to know
How many years of purchase, and what price,
The promised favour of a prince is worth.
    Sci. Nay, sir, the duke Alfonso of Ferrara
Is more than a mere prince; he is the friend
Of art and poesy, the comrade sworn
Of artists and of poets, who with him,
And his like-minded sister, find themselves
More honoured for the honour they can give
Than high-born lords for honour that they claim.
    Lau. This duke hath then a sister?
    Sci.   Know you not?
The Princess Leonora—one who sets
By poets and the poet's art such store,
She might well-nigh be deemed their patron saint.
    Tas. [*To* LAURA.] You see, you see—I shall not
        lack for friends.
    Lau. [*To* SCIPIO.] And is this princess, sir, as
        fair of face
As by her birth she should be, and the praise
You put upon her?
    Sci.   Ay, as fair as wise—
In brief, so graced and graceful in all things
That though she were not sister of the duke,

Still of his court she were the brightest star.

   Lau. In truth a lady of rare excellence.

                          [*Trumpets sound at a distance.*

   Sci. Hark there! the trumpets of the Cardinal.
[*To* TASSO.] Hold yourself ready, friend.

   Tas.   'Tis time to part.
But ere I part, Signor Fabrizio,

            [*Advancing with* LAURA *and* FABRIZIO.
Give me one thing to make my parting glad,
As a fair sunset promising fair dawn—
Your leave to call your daughter my betrothed.

   Fab. Your pardon, sir; that cannot be as yet.
First schedule me the profits of the trade
You have seen fit to choose, and bring me proof
Of what the favour of a duke is worth,
And to your suit I'll give attentive ear.
Till then I do forbid it, and advise
That to my daughter now you say farewell
As though for the last time, since 'tis my will
That neither with your presence nor your pen
Her peace be troubled more. [*Turns away, leaving*
       TASSO *and* LAURA *still in front.*

   Lau.   'Tis very hard—
But in your thoughts, love, call me your betrothed,
For so I promise will I always be
Will you but promise too, and ne'er forget.

   Tas. With my whole being I promise. See, let
      this
Be our betrothal-ring.

[*Taking off a ring, and putting it on her finger.*
Lau. The only one
That e'er shall bind my faith—and while 'tis mine
So long shall I be yours. [*Trumpets sound nearer.*
What! there again?
So soon to part!
Tas. 'Tis for my good and thine.
Clau. [*Aside to* LORENZO.] I'm gladder yet than e'er I thought to be
That Heav'n made thee no poet.
Sci. [*To* TASSO.] See, 'tis time—
The banners of the Cardinal!
Greg. [*Aside.*] At last
For the pasty and for peace.
[*A gate at the back of the stage is thrown open, showing beyond a procession, with the* CARDINAL OF ESTE *borne in a litter. An Attendant of the Cardinal advances.*
Att. His Eminence
The Cardinal of Este summons forth
The Signor Tasso.
Tas. In humility
I am ready to attend him where he will.
Signor Fabrizio, friends all, farewell.
[*To* LAURA.] Lady, I kiss your hand, and crave to keep
A place in your remembrance.
Lau. Sir, farewel;
You have what you have asked.

[TASSO *advances to the* CARDINAL, *to whom he makes obeisance, then takes his place in the procession, which, at a sign from the* CARDINAL, *moves forward.*
Gone! he is gone!
[*Sinks into* CLAUDIA'S *arms. The Curtain falls.*

END OF ACT I.

ACT II.

SCENE I.

Ferrara. A Hall in the Duke's Palace.

FRANCESCO *and* MADDALO *discovered speaking together.*
Enter ASCANIO.

Asc. Signor Francesco, Signor Maddalo—
Good-morrow, sirs. What! has his grace not bid
Your presence at the feast?
    Fran.   Nay, not to-day.
Hath he not yours, Signor Ascanio?
    Asc. Nay, not to-day. You know the feast to-day
Is for the new-come nuncio and his train,
And where so many strangers crowd the board
We more familiar guests must deem ourselves
Honoured in being chosen to make room.
    Fran. So say I too. 'Tis e'en as though the duke
Asked us to give him help in welcoming
His and Ferrara's friends.
    Mad.   And then of feasts
We have seen so many that to 'scape this one
Is as a kind of boon.

Fran. O quite a boon.
Asc. The very word.
Fran.   Besides, we have compassed leave
To sit in the loft above the banquet-hall,
Where we shall have full view. Will you come too?
   Asc. Say you full view? Why then, methinks I will.
   Mad. Nor shall we lack wherewith to drink the toasts.
See here.   [*Showing a bottle from his pocket.*
   Asc. Kind friends, I'll go where'er you please.
                    [*Trumpets sound.*
Hark, they set forth unto the feast e'en now.
   Mad. And pass this way?
   Asc.   Look yonder where they come.
   Fran. Is that the nuncio with whom the duke
And the duke's sister speak?
   Asc.   Ay, ay. Stand close.

[*Trumpets. Enter* DUKE *and* LEONORA, *with the Papal Nuncio, followed by a train of courtiers, including* TASSO, *and of attendants of the Nuncio, among whom is* SCIPIO GONZAGA. *They cross the stage, and go out at the side opposite to that at which they have entered.*

   Fran. So! see you that the Signor Tasso goes
'Mong the invited guests?
   Asc.   I see in truth—
And marvel much that such as he find room

While men of like account to you, and you,
Are left to stand outside.
  Fran.   The very thing
I was about to speak of you, dear friend.
  Mad. See what it is to tickle on the ear
A duke and a duke's sister.
  Fran.   Hush! Yet this
I'll say, were I the duke, he should have leave
To laud me as he would, but not to write
Love-sonnets to my sister.
  Asc.   Certain 'tis
He hath writ praises of her hair and eyes
That, had he said, he would have had to rue.
But, being rhymed and copied fairly out,
They have earned him nought but thanks.
  Mad.   My marvel is
The princess will endure it.
  Asc.   O but ladies
Will endure much that way. Shall we see more?
Where is the vantage-place you told me of?
  Fran. I'll lead you, friends. Come, come, we will have sport,
Albeit we cannot jingle words like some.
  Mad. And who shall say but if we tried we might?
        [*Exeunt.*

Enter TASSO *and* SCIPIO GONZAGA.

Tas. I tell you, it was purposed—and by Heaven
I will not bear it.
Sci. Nay, I cannot deem
'Twas purposed, friend, indeed.
Tas. Be 't as it may;
Below my wonted place I will not sit.
But with intent 'twas done, with set intent
To badge me for a hireling.
Sci. You must think
That when so many noble guests are met
'Tis hard to portion unto each his place
Without offending some.
Tas. I am noble too,
And am moreover Tasso—nor will brook
To be made less than equal with the best.
Sci. I am sorry this should chance upon the day
That after such long sev'rance brings us first
To meet again—a meeting whereupon
I had set such store that chiefly for its sake
Ferrara sees me in the nuncio's train.
Tas. Best friend, I know—and sorry I no less;
But 'tis no fault of mine.
Sci. I had been told
That unto you the duke was wondrous kind.
Tas. Kind! Ay, in truth 'tis a kind duke to all
Who make a part of his own glory—kind

To the Court poet, kind to the Court fool,
And the Court dwarf—most kind.
 Sci.   Nay, but I thought
That unto you he had been kind as prince
To his most honoured subject—kind as friend
Unto his chosen friend.
 Tas.   Say he is kind,
Have I not proved me worthy of my hire,
And in requital of his bread and meat
Stuffed him enough with praise, the food he loves?
Have I not set his name so in the front
Of my new work and greatest that for ever
'Tis branded with his brand? have I not ridden
My fancy lame to find fit metaphors
To honour him—and turn-and-turn-about
Hailed him as Jove, and Mars? What would he more?
 Sci. O patience; this is frenzy.
 Tas.   Patience, yea;
That man needs patience to whom Nature gives
A gift that Fortune grudges, who is born
Unto a heritage he cannot win
Saving with help he loathes. O curse of fate,
That made me greater, and yet so much less,
Than those poor sceptred puppets!
 Sci.   I know not
If most I grieve, or wonder. I had heard
You stood in the inmost friendship of the duke
And of his sister—and to find you now
So fierce in anger 'gainst them——

Tas.   Not 'gainst her!
O never think my lips could frame of her
A word unworthy, or my brain a thought—
Her whose mild presence, shining through the dark
By its own brightness, as a fair saint's head,
Hath been in this drear place my only light.
   Sci. You praise her high.
   Tas.   And if my praise could reach
As high as Heaven's roof it would not top
Her loftier deserving.
   Sci.   Were it not
I have a nearer knowledge than most men
Of you and your concernments, I should fear
That that report was true which I have heard,
But only smiled to hear.
   Tas.   And what report?
O I know well they are busy with my name.
   Sci. Why, that the poet-homage which you bring
The princess in your verse but masquerades
The love of a man's heart. Yet would I hope
That thus it cannot be.
   Tas.   So—this hath travelled
As far as you, and found, I see, with you
A traveller's welcome. Love! you think that she,
And I, and love, are three that may be linked
In the same breath together? *I* love *her!*
You are pleased to say so.
   Sci.   I could well-nigh deem
You found more pleasure in these words than I.

Tas. Because they show me what those men must be
Who, if they see a worshipper at prayer
To his Madonna, needs must think he loves
Heav'n's queen in fleshly fashion.   But I hold
That Heav'n, though Heav'n is high, may be adored
Beneath the lowliest roof without offence.

Sci. Right glad I am to find that thus it stands;
For O, my friend, for an unarmoured heart
There's deadly danger in a woman barred
By policy from mating, yet by blood,
And vanity, and heavy-hanging hours,
Pricked on to play at love.

Tas.   Which of my foes
Hath told you of this way to make me mad?
O pardon me, you are not one of those;
But you should know how far beyond the bounds
Of all things possible this danger is
Whereof you warn me so unneedfully.

Sci. You mean because I know you are betrothed?
This had I not forgot.

Tas.   What! I betrothed?
You heard the father say it could not be.

Sci. But heard you promise to account yourself
In your own heart betrothed.

Tas.   I promised—true;
And keep my promise still—albeit indeed
Made so long since that like enough 'tis now
By all save me forgot.   But get you back
To the feast; you will be missed.

Sci. It matters not.
For the feast I have no heart.
　　Tas. Nay, but I pray——
If you must know, by your imaginings,
So foolish and unbased, you have hurt me sore,
And I must be alone ere I can quench
The fever you have lit. Beseech you then
Back to your place, nor give to me more heed.
　　Sci. Indeed I see here can I do no good. [*Exit.*
　　Tas. Love! I know well myself it is not love,
That it dare not be love—though others see
No strangeness in the thought; but these would see
No strangeness in a mortal stretching forth
His arms to clasp a goddess—or perchance
In her requiting him with love for love,
As once the silver-footed queen of night
Stole down the path that leads from heav'n to earth
To kiss the Latmian sleeper. Fables all—
I will no more of them; they turn my brain.
　　　　　[MADDALO *is heard singing behind the scene.*
　　Mad. [*Singing.*] *Where wine is a-flowing,*
　　　　　With glasses to catch,
　　　　　There hearts are a-glowing,
　　　　　And noses to match.

Enter ASCANIO, FRANCESCO, *and* MADDALO, *the last still singing.*

　　　　　Where wine is a-flowing,
　　　　　With glasses to catch——

How does it go?
   Tas.   I'll hence.   No, I will stay,
Or they would deem I fear.
   Mad.   I have it now—
[*Singing*]   *There hearts are a-glowing,*
            And noses to match.
Who's this? the Signor Tasso?
   Tas.   Sir, the same—
Unless I am drunk, and have forgot myself.
   Mad. Mean you to call me drunk?
   Tas.   Nay, on my life—
Why should I? there's no need.
   Mad.   Be thankful, sir,
You have not said it, for whoe'er should put
That word on me, him would I quarrel with.
   Tas. And with none here I would quarrel for the
      world.
   Mad. So much the better.
   Asc.   A good friendly soul.
   Fran. Friendlier indeed than e'er I took him for.
In faith, we will not quarrel.
   Tas.   Heav'n forbid;
They must come near who quarrel—and besides,
It is the curse of quarrels they are apt
To lead to reconcilements.
   Fran.   I doubt not
Your meaning's good, although sometimes, as now,
I fathom you not fully.
   Tas.   Like enough.

Fran. But let that be, and give us leave to say
How glad we are to find occasion thus
To tell you how we grieved to see the slight
They put on you to-day.
  Tas.   What mean you here?
  Fran. Setting your seat at bottom of the board—
O how we grieved!
  Asc.   A monstrous slight indeed;
You did well not to bear it.
  Tas.   Nor will bear
Your pity now, be sure.
  Asc.   What! take offence
Because we say in all sincerity——
  Tas. Sincerity! From your sincerity
The saints deliver me and all good men.
Sincerity! a screen you sit behind
To play what tricks you will. I pray you, none
Of your sincerity.
  Mad.   And if not that—
'Tis a long word, and so I say it not—
If none of that, what would you?
  Tas.   Nought of yours—
Unless indeed your absence.
  Mad.   To my ears
It sounds as though the paper-scratching fellow
Desired us to be gone.
  Fran.   That well may be;
He knows that we are gentlemen—unversed
In the weapons of his warfare.

Tas. [*Touching his sword.*] You may choose
Your weapon if you will.
Fran. Ay, for you know
That here within the palace of the duke,
Where none dare draw, 'tis safe to let me choose.
Mad. Ha! ha! you have him there.
Tas. But I dare draw,
And in the palace of the duke chastise
Uncourtly manners—thus.
[*Striking* FRANCESCO *with the flat of his sword.*
Fran. If this were not
The palace of the duke——
Tas. And thus. [*Striking* MADDALO.
Mad. Nay then,
I'll fight though this were fifty palaces.
[*Attacks* TASSO, *who defends himself.*
Fran. And so will I, now that I think of it.
A man of honour may not bear a blow.
[*Makes a pass at* TASSO, *who turns upon him furiously.*
Tas. Heel-snapping cur, there's for thee.
[*Strikes the sword out of* FRANCESCO'S *hand, then goes on fighting with* MADDALO.
Fran. If 'twere not
The palace of the duke——
Asc. Ay, ay, we know—
But since it is the palace of the duke,
Were it not good to give his highness word
Of how his poet-pet doth bear himself?

Fran. Well thought of; he shall have the news forthwith.
Till I bring help, stay you as witness here.
   Asc. I will, but pray you haste.
                             [*Exit* FRANCESCO.
                             Poor Maddalo—
He will be murdered, sure.   Dear gentlemen——
   Tas. What! you too, greybeard!
   Asc.   O no, no, not I.
Do as you will for me; I meant no harm—
A greybeard, as you say—a poor old man.

[TASSO *and* MADDALO *continue to fight, until presently Enter* DUKE, *with Courtiers.*

   Duke. Peace ho! put up your swords, nor dare profane
These precincts more. Now fetch your breath, and say
How comes it this presumptuous affront
Is laid on me and on my sov'reignty?
They tell me, Tasso, 'twas your sword that first,
With sudden and most traitor-like assault,
Broke up a peaceful converse; then you first
I charge to clear yourself if clear you can.
   Tas. I will not say, my lord, but that my steel
Came soonest from its scabbard—yet methinks
Constrained thereto by insult of such sort
That the aggressor's blame was none of mine.
   Duke. What blame may lie with others I will weigh
And punish in its turn; but since you own

To have made so grave a trespass 'gainst my state
Of sov'reign and of host (nor is it now
Your humours first disturb me), I must deem
'Tis time you leave a town and court wherein
A prince who is your friend with all his pains
So little can content you. I am sorry
That this must be, but judge it best for all.
 Tas. And of all best for me. Think not there's need
To make the flavour of dismissal sweet
By saying you are sorry. I was held
Bondsman, and now am free—and once being free
Will rather hide me in some wilderness,
With stones my daily bread and sand my drink,
Than play the courtier in a court again.
And gladly as the new-redeemèd soul,
Set loose from fiery torment, bathes and dives
In heav'n's cool blue, so I in liberty,
Being 'scaped from out this place that was my hell—
The house of bondage where I lay in chains,
And gaolers mocked me — the loath'd torture-room——

 [*He pauses suddenly, and gazes at* LEONORA, *who enters with* LIVIA, ANGELICA, *and other Ladies.*

 Leo. O what is this? I charge you, brother, say.
Some ill hath chanced, I know.
 Duke.   Nay, here is nought;
Only the Signor Tasso who unloads

His soul of some of that great freight of joy
Wherewith 'tis filled at parting from our court.

    Leo. At parting from our court! and who hath said
Such parting is to be? and who agreed
To aught so wildly spoken? I must fear
You are too yielding, brother, for a prince;
See, I am but a woman, yet will deal
Herein with more imperial voice than yours,
For if to me the Signor Tasso says
He thus would rob our court, I answer back
He must not, shall not, cannot.

    Tas.   But I must;
Your brother's self hath said it, and I must.
Forgive, and let me go.

    Leo.   My brother's self!
O something here worse than I thought hath been.
And stay! [*Looking at Tasso.*] is that not blood you seek to hide?
You are wounded; how comes this?

    Duke.   From the arrogance
That turned my court to a place of private brawl.

    Tas. From the arrogance that others used on me,
And which in any house or presence soe'er
I was not framed to bear.

    Duke.   So—do you hear
How little sorry——

    Leo.   Ah! no more just now—
Or both might say in heat what both when cool

Would fain take back and could not. [*To* Tasso.
 You are hurt;
Go and make haste to have your wound bound up,
And then return to me, and give me here
Some quiet speech with you.
 Tas. Nay, what hath been
Not even you can make undone again.
'Twere best I came no more.
 Leo. And yet I pray,
Promise you will return; here will I wait.
 Tas. You ask me; 'tis enough. Doubt not, I'll
 come. [*Exit.*
 Leo. [*Advancing with the* Duke, *while the others
 stand apart.*
Brother, be well advised. What! have you been
Throughout his evil days the patron-friend
Of the age's chiefest poet, and when such
At last all hail him, will you now fall back,
And let the golden harvest of renown
His gratitude should bring to you and yours
Be gathered in by others? Give me leave
To be ambassador 'twixt you and him,
And all shall yet go well.
 Duke. He hath tired me out.
His whims and freaks and varying appetites—
Now craving homage, now on watch to catch
A flavour of affront, as though nought else
Had taste or relish in't—these thousand humours
And daintinesses changed from day to day

Are past all bearing.
 Leo.   You have borne them long;
'Twere pity if you lost your patience now,
When he so soon will give unto the world
His poem of poems, his "Jerusalem,"
Whereon, as on a monument, is carved
Your and your house's glory. And remember,
The hand that wrote may blot.
 Duke.   Ay, that is true,
And hard it were to lose what in more ways
Than I can count I have paid for.
 Leo.   Then, good brother,
Give me full power to deal, and you shall find
That, on his part, the rage that leapt so high
Will at my voice fall down, and be as tame
As the caged lion when the keeper comes
Who once hath quelled him.
 Duke.   Even there you touch
A reason weightier perchance than all
To make me deem it best he should be gone.
 Leo. What reason may that be? if not too weighty
To be delivered by a mortal tongue.
 Duke. Know you not, sister, that report makes bold
To say—he loves you?
 Leo.   There now, only see
The ungallant creatures that these brothers are!
And if report spoke true, would it be then
A thing so mightily to wonder at?
 Duke. Nay, but as natural as nature's self

That made fair women fair. Yet if it chanced
That, moved by your own tenderness of heart,
Or blinded by the brightness of his fame,
You—you——
    Leo.   If I returned him love for love?
O speak it boldly out; 'tis all as well
To insult me with your words as with your looks,
And pauses, and throat-clearings. Though indeed
I scarce can marvel that you fear to tell
A sister and a princess of your house
How immeasurably lowlier you deem
Her spirit than her birth. What have I done
To show that I forget my ancestors
Were royal e'en as yours?
    Duke. [*Kissing her hand.*] O truly nought—
Nor ever will, nor can. Forgive me, sweet;
You have made me see my fault.
    Leo.   And with our poet
You will not fear to let me have my way?
    Duke. Do even as you will; you are my sister,
In whom I wholly trust.
    Leo.   Why, that is well.
Now pray you hence; I look for him full soon,
And to prevail must deal with him alone.
    Duke. Prevail you will, I know. Come, gentlemen;
We'll to our guests again. [*Exit, with Courtiers.*
    Leo.   So think I too.
    [*Turning to her Ladies.*] Well, girls, what do you
    there? How! like scared birds,

Still twitt'ring o'er your fright? Yet will I own
I was myself affrighted when I heard,
As we came in, what fiery wrath possessed
The Signor Tasso. Happy 'twas for us
He seemed to hold our presence in more awe
Than we did his, and, as you saw, grew tame
As though we were a band of Amazons
Rather than gentle ladies. Did you mark
How quickly he was quelled?
 Liv.   I marked indeed—
And would have wondered knew I not the cause.
 Leo. The cause—what cause, so please you? But
   you mean
His reverence for ladies?
 Liv.   Ladies—nay;
One lady 'twas who curbed him, and no more.
 Ang. I never saw the like. The rage at once
Went from his eyes, and to your highness' face
They turned and gazed content, as though 'twere food
They had been fasting for.
 Liv.   I'd give ten years
For but a day's such power upon a man.
 Ang. And such a man—a man who on the beauty
He loves to gaze at can bestow the gift
Of an immortal life.
 Leo.   A foolish pair
Of maidens are you both, who think each word
A poet writes for sake of rhythm and rhyme
Must needs be true.

Liv.   'Tis written on his face
As well as in his verse that he is burned
With inner fires that would consume him quite,
If awe and worship of your royal state
Had not already turned him half to stone.
　Ang. And that now e'en the stony part of him
Begins to catch are many signs of late.
　　Leo. Hush, hush, he comes. Peace with your foolishness.
　　Ang. Madam, I am dumb. But look at him and say,
For all his paleness, if he doth not burn
From head to foot.

Enter TASSO, *his arm bound up. The Ladies retire to the back part of the stage.*

　　Tas.   Your highness bade me come
To see you ere I parted, and I come.
　　Leo. I give you thanks for so much courtesy.
I pray you sit. [*Seating herself on a sofa, and motioning him to a place beside her.*] O I must have it so;
Your wound hath left you faint. Sit, and for once
Forget I am a princess—as indeed
I oft-times would I could myself forget.
Sir, by the duke my brother I am bid
Deliver you a message——But you breathe
As quick as though in fever.
　　Tas.   Nay, 'tis nought—

The wound, e'en as you say; but all your words
I am able well to note.
  Leo.   My brother then
Would have me tell you, as from friend to friend,
That he repents his heat, and doth entreat you
To honour with your presence still his court,
Where what you have found amiss shall be redressed,
And who have wronged you forced to sue their peace.
All this he would have said himself, but feared
Yet further to offend, and so chose me,
A guiltless herald, unto whom he thinks
You cannot well deny the prayer he makes—
And I with him—Stay at Ferrara still.
  Tas. I must not.
  Leo.   Must not!
  Tas.   Dare not, call it then.
Ask of me aught but this, and I will give;
This only can I not.
  Leo.   You are resolved
To go—to go, and never see us more?
  Tas. E'en so—to go, and never see you more.
  Leo. I had not thought you could be thus unkind.
And whither will you go? where is't you think
To find new friends who will be more your friends
Than those you leave behind, who more than they
Will have your good at heart, or more than they
The power to serve you, and to spread your name,
And your great poem's name, to the utmost edge
Of Fame's broad sea, wherein so much is cast

One round of ripples blots the other out
Ere it hath time to widen?
   Tas.   My great poem
Shall help the convent fire, when the lay-brother
Finds that his wood is damp—and I myself
Shall have no name but that which I may choose
For my companion-monks to call me by.
Ay, lady, monks—these are henceforth my friends,
And saints my patrons, and the court they serve—
The court of Heav'n—my court to which I look
To help me and protect. For this it can—
It only—and it will, if rightly asked,
And give me peace and rest, and keep me safe.
   Leo. Is this in earnest? You to be no more
Tasso, but only one of many monks?
   Tas. In earnest, madam—yea, as death itself.
   Leo. Why then, in no less earnest let me say
You have no right to rob the world of you,
No right to make a lazy suicide
Of your own glory and immortal name
Only because you are tired. Pray pardon me
That thus I dare to chide; but in my voice
Think that you hear the world that you would
       wrong—
Think that in me Fame speaks, Fame who for you
Hath ne'er had aught but kindness, and is now
With wounding scorn requited.
   Tas.   O most strange!
You say that you are Fame?

Leo. I said I spoke
As Fame would speak. What is there here so
 strange?
Tas. Long ago, lady, even on that night
After I saw you first, I had a dream.
Methought you sat high raised upon a throne,
And I, as fitting was, low 'neath your feet,
When graciously you bent, and in my hand
Gave something—this I knew, though with mine eyes
I could not see it or with fingers feel.
And then you smiled, but with that smile it seemed
My sleeping fancy had outwrought itself,
For I awoke. And as I woke, the thought
Came to my mind—whence I know not, unless
I brought it with me from the realm of sleep—
That I had even then been face to face
With the genius of my fame, that you indeed,
And fame, for me were one.
 Leo. And to be this
Would please me better than to give the law
Unto an empire. I beseech you, strive
To think of me thus always, and the thought
Will bring its own fulfilment. See, I now
Make my first act of office, and command
That, as you tender Fame and her rewards,
You here shall stay to reap them.
 Tas. Yet I once
Was warned—and warned by one who wished me
 well—

Fame is not peace, nor yet true happiness.
I heeded little then—but now begin
To think that she was wise who spoke those words.
  Leo. She! who is she that is so fortunate
To be by you deemed wise, and whose advice,
I needs must own, doth savour of a judgment
So ancient and discreet?
  Tas.   One that I knew
At Mantua once. But, lady——
  Leo.   I have heard
That you were once in love at Mantua.
Aha! I see; she that you speak of now
Is that same Laura you so worshipped there,
And praised in sonnets and in madrigals.
Is this not so?
  Tas.   'Twas but of what she said
I spoke—not of herself.
  Leo.   You must not think
That such sweet rhymes as those have been by us
Not noted and admired—right tuneful rhymes;
Albeit perchance a trifle too unmellow,
And tasting of the wood. But tell me now,
Is 't true (for what you poets say none know
If it be meant for music or for truth),
Is 't true this Laura was by you so loved?
  Tas. I ne'er have said but as I think. Ay, then
I thought I loved her—then, when she loved me.
  Leo. But now I see that she no longer loves?
  Tas. Her father was against me, and her nature

Submiss and dutiful; if she was told
She must forget me, she would strive to obey.
But with our theme her name hath nought to do—
Nor know I how it came in our discourse.

Leo. Because you told me what wise prudent saws
She spoke of fame, and peace, and happiness.
But let me now tell you, if e'er she sought
To pluck you back from seeking as you could
The glory that is yours by natural right,
Not only hath she now forgot to love,
But loved you truly never.

Tas.   So in sooth
One well might deem. And yet methinks she did.

Leo. But I say no—and you may take my word.
Who truly loves is proud of what she loves,
And hungry for more food to feed her pride;
And so would she by whom you were loved indeed
Charge you to set your glory in the front
Of all your strivings, bid you follow it
As your chief good at any price soe'er,
And counsel you—e'en as I counsel now.

Tas. As you—as she—O say again—again—
Before this whirl that's in my brain shall stop
My sense from understanding.

Leo.   What is this
Moves you so strangely? But I'll say again
If so you will. I counsel you to stay
Here at Ferrara, and to force from Fame
The birthright that she owes you.

Tas. And e'en thus
You think would counsel those who—care for me—
Who—who—I would say care for me?
  Leo. E'en thus
Would counsel all your friends—or all at least
So much your friends as I.
  Tas. You—you—is 't so?
You give yourself that name?
  Leo. Why, surely yes—
If there is need to give myself a name
I thought was mine before. But now I see;
You doubt my friendship, and that doubt it is
Which makes your heart so obstinate to my prayer.
  Tas. Nay, nay, no longer obstinate. I obey—
Will stay—will do all things you bid me do—
If 'twere with my life's blood to lay the dust
Below your sov'reign feet.
  Leo. I will not ask
So much as that. I do but bid you stay,
And for your yielding thank you from my heart.
But with your wound I see you are fevered much;
You must go rest awhile. And since you are pleased
To treat me as a queen, I give you here
My hand to kiss at parting, as a seal
Of your renewed allegiance and my grace.
  [*Rising and offering him her hand.*
  Tas. [*Half rising, and seizing her hand, which he covers with kisses.*] This hand—her hand—at last.
  O pardon me—

I am ailing—give me help.
> [*Falls back swooning on the sofa.*

Leo.   Girls, hear you not?
He calls for help; make haste. Angelica,
Hold you his head, and you, good Livia, look
To the bandage of his wound. Now is 't not
    strange?
I did but let him have my hand to kiss,
And even at that moment must his wound
Have broken forth afresh.

Ang.   Not strange at all—
Though plainly proving that for him there dwells
In the white softness of your highness' hand
Some mortal magic.

Leo.   So 'twould well-nigh seem.
> [*The Curtain falls,* LEONORA *still standing, while her Ladies busy themselves round* TASSO.

END OF ACT II.

ACT III.

SCENE I.

Near Ferrara. The Garden of the Duke's Summer Palace of Belriguardo.

Enter TASSO.

Tas. O pleasant Belriguardo, place of peace
And holy quiet, where the sunlight seems,
As on the lawn it lies, to have fall'n asleep,
And left nought near it well awake, save only
The fountain's dropping music, and the shadows
That flit beneath the trees—how have I longed
For thee, and thy deep groves, and tangled bowers,
And mossy coolnesses! And thou wilt keep
The promise of thy beauty, thou wilt help me
To find that dear occasion that in vain
I sought for 'midst the turmoil of the court—
The time and place when I with her alone
May speak, and hear her answer. Sure methinks
Here nature's very self will plead my cause,
And tune her heart to pity, so that more
She will not shun me. Not that willingly

She shunned me ever—nay, 'twas but because
In the city she belongs not to herself,
But lives, as 'twere, in the eyes of all the world;
And sometimes, in despite of all the world,
She hath said and looked such things as unto one
Who had staked a little less of love than I
Were certitude enough.   But I have given
So much, no common surety serves my turn;
And even from her lips, yea, with her lips,
I must have proof I am blest, before I cease
To be in torment.

Enter ASCANIO, FRANCESCO, MADDALO, LIVIA, *and*
ANGELICA.

                        What! in this place too
Those gnats must still be buzzing?   [*Going*.
    Liv.   Stay, sir, stay.
Too late to 'scape; we see you.
    Tas.   Madam——
    Liv.   Fie!
The uncivil manners! for you saw us well,
Even as we saw you.
    Ang.   Uncourtly knight!
    Tas. Uncourtly! give me not so hard a word.
I saw—but saw not that you saw I saw.
    Liv. Why, here is quibbling!
    Tas.   If I have offended,
I am obedient now.   What may there be
That you would say to me?
    Liv.   O many things.

Well, first to ask wherefore you went not forth
Unto the chase this morning with the rest.
You were sore missed, I promise you.
　　Ang.　　　　　　　　　All saw
And felt your absence.
　　Fran. [*Aside to* ASCANIO *and* MADDALO.] That did
　　　I indeed,
And fared the better for it.
　　Asc. [*Aside to* FRANCESCO.] And I too;
The duke twice spoke to me, and once he smiled.
[*Aloud.*] O sir, we felt it all most sensibly.
　　Mad. [*Aside.*] And wished 'twould last for ever.
　　　[*Aloud.*] As he says,
Most sensibly we felt it.
　　Tas.　　　　　　　Sure I am
All that you feel you feel most sensibly.
I thank you much; but, as it chanced, to-day
I had no care for sport.
　　Liv.　　　　　　　The princess too
Missed you, and wondered.
　　Tas.　　　　　　　She! I was to blame;
I should have gone, but knew not she would mark——
She was not angered, think you?
　　Liv.　　　　　　　Angered! nay—
She knows too well unto what use you put
Your leisure, to begrudge it. Tell me now,
Tell me—all here are friends—when shall the world
Have your great poem?
　　Tas.　　　　　　You are certain then
She doth not blame me?

Liv.   O for that I'll vouch.
But of your poem, sir; I had been told
'Twas finished; sure 'tis most unkind to make
So many longings wait.
　　Tas.   'Tis finished, madam,
E'en as the steel is finished whereupon
The anvil's work is done—in form and shape—
But must be wrought to smoothness ere I dare
Wear it in sight of men.
　　Liv.   Yet would they well
Forgive a spot or two.
　　Tas.   But not so well
Could I forgive myself.
　　Liv.   Why then at least
Please you make smooth with all the speed you can,
For the world waits, and waits impatiently.
　　Tas. I will obey you, madam, even now.　[*Going.*
　　Liv. Whither away? Sir, sir!
　　Tas.   You bade me work,
And poets, as you know, must work alone.
It is their only privilege.　　　　　　　　[*Exit.*
　　Liv.   One word!
Nay, he is gone. What pity 'tis these poets—
So all-adorable in other ways—
Should be at times so absent in their moods,
So strange and sudden!
　　Ang.   O 'tis grievous quite—
The only fault they have!
　　Asc.   Then be content

With those that are not poets, but will never
Be absent, you being present.
    Liv.   In yourselves
You are well enough, but with a stroke of the pen
You cannot make our names for ever live.
Would he had stayed—I was about to beg
For a new sonnet.
    Ang.   Even so was I.
    Fran. I marvel how you care to have the droppings
Of a pen that to another gives its best.
    Mad. And what are then these sonnets? twisted rhymes,
With sense and sentences turned inside out,
To tell you that no more Angelica
You should be called, but angel. As for that,
Why, I could call you angel if you will.
    Ang. But if you called me so, good Maddalo,
No creature were the wiser.
    Liv.   Who are those
That come this way, and look around with eyes
So seeking and unsure? the man by his garb
A citizen, and, most certain, strangers both.
    Mad. A right fair damsel, be she who she may.
I'll offer her my service.

            Enter FABRIZIO *and* LAURA.

                Is there aught,
Lady, that I may help you in? I pray you,
Command me as you will.

Fab.   Indeed, good sir,
We are beholden much, for, as I fear,
Albeit not transgressors by our wont,
We have wandered further than our right allowed.
    Mad. O take no pains to excuse; so bright a dame
As your—your—but I know not how to call
Your fair companion?
    Fab.   'Tis my daughter, sir.
    Mad. Thanks — as your daughter, hath a right to go
Where'er she hath a mind.
    Fab.   We are most happy
To find such kindness here, where, as you see,
We are but new and strange, being indeed
No more than travellers, who so oft have heard
Of this famed Belriguardo, with its palace
And wondrous gardens, that we have a little,
Turned from our way to judge them for ourselves.
    Mad. To the gardens let me give you welcome now.
For the palace, I must fear I have not power
To bid you enter in, since for a while
The duke and princess make their dwelling there.
    Fab. We know; 'tis not an hour since at the gate
Of the park we stood and watched them with their train
Returning from the chase. But with the gardens
We can content us well. Right fair, in sooth—
And I who say it understand a little

The laying out of gardens.
Mad.   I would hope
They have your daughter's commendation too,
Though yet she hath not spoken.
Lau.   Surely, sir;
Nay, who that could but look would not commend?
Liv. And that doth mean the lady much commends,
For truly she hath looked, and looked again,
As though till now her eyes had never seen.
Lau. What! have I seemed unmannered? pray forgive
One who is new to travel, and at home
Used but to homely ways.
Liv.   O my dear child,
No need to explain. [*Aside to* ANGELICA, ASCANIO, *and* FRANCESCO.] Did I not tell you so?
Ang. [*Aside to* LIVIA.] Nay, but I saw it too.
What are the eyes
Of that poor Maddalo made of?
Lau.   Lady, say,
Is't in your knowledge if to Belriguardo
All of the court have followed?
Liv.   All—e'en so.
Why should you ask?
Lau. For nought—nay, nought. You, madam,
Are of the court, methinks, and all else here?
Liv. Ay, surely. I would hope that in your sight
We seem not quite uncourtly.
Mad.   We not only,

Fair one, are of the court, but some of us
In high esteem at court.

Lau.   Why then, belike——
[*Aside to* FABRIZIO.] Father, ask you; I cannot.

Fab.   Since it seems,
My lords and ladies, you are of the court—
As truly is but fitting—it may be
You have some knowledge of a Signor Tasso,
Who, as they say, is much about the duke.

Liv. A Signor Tasso! Where was this man born
That for *a* Signor Tasso he must ask?
As though there were a hundred Signor Tassos,
'Mong whom, with some slight pains, and questioning
Of Christian name and tint of hair and eyes,
We might at last pick forth the one he means.

Mad. Well, we have sometimes cause enough to think
There are a hundred—Signor Tasso this,
And Signor Tasso that; at every turn
We are met by Signor Tasso.

Fran.   Very true;
There seems a plague of Tassos.

Asc.   Whereunto
I echo in response—A plague of Tasso.

Liv. [*To* FABRIZIO.] But let me tell you, friend, though of the name
There lived a hundred, yea, a thousand here,
In the world's count will ne'er be more than one,
And he so great that now and in all time

He needs no style but—Tasso.
 Lau. [*Aside to* FABRIZIO.] Hear you that?
Father—you hear?
 Fab.   And of this Tasso then,
Can any tell me if that tale be true
Which goes abroad—that he is deep in love
With the duke's sister?
 Liv.   Sir!—Is this not strange?
I have forgot my fan. Angelica,
Be pleased to lend me yours. O the brave fan!
In faith, most choicely painted—and for carving,
I never saw the like. Francesco, look.
 Fran. Rare workmanship indeed. May I be suffered
To play the part of Zephyrus? [*Taking the fan.*
 Mad. [*To* FABRIZIO.] Good sir,
Were it not better be more circumspect
In the framing of your questions?
 Fab. [*Looking at* LAURA.] That is true;
You well remind me. I will ask you then,
Think you the sister of the duke loves him,
And seeks to entice him on?
 Liv. [*To* FRANCESCO, *taking the fan from him.*] Nay, in good sooth,
I will not tire you longer. See with thanks
Your fan again, Angelica. I'll in,
And seek some shade; here doth it grow too hot.
 Asc. Ay, hotter ev'ry minute.
 Ang.   Not indeed

Longer to be endured.
  Fran.   Lean on my arm.
  Mad. Forget not me, I pray; I'll bear your fan.
[*Aside, looking at* LAURA.] Pity that Nature gave so
      fair a maid
So indiscreet a father.
                [*Exeunt all but* FABRIZIO *and* LAURA.
  Fab.   Well, if these
Be courtly manners, I will keep mine own.
Child, how you tremble! And so pale! Please
      Heaven
You fall not ill again.
  Lau.   Fear not for that.
  Fab. On your sick-bed you promised me with vows
That if·I brought you hither it should serve
To cure you quite; but now I doubt the med'cine
Will rather hurt than heal.
  Lau.   It shall not hurt,
And it shall heal; believe.
  Fab.   Remember well
Our bargain, that if hither you should come
To search for truth yourself, whate'er you found
You would with patience take—ay, e'en the proof
That he hath done with you, and turned his love,
And his billing and his cooing, to this woman
They call a princess.
  Lau.   Father! But such proof
Is not yet found; you have no right till then
To say such things of him.

Fab.   I do but try
To hold you to remembrance of your bond.
I on my part have promised that if true
We find him still, and slandered by report,
I give him you, and with you all I prize.
This promise will I keep; but keep you yours—
That if we find him false you are content
To be my child, and think of him no more.

   Lau. I promised, and I promise yet again—
To speak of him no more, or wish for him;
Yea, for your sake to be to you and the world
As though I had wished never.

   Fab.   There's my girl!
I know you now once more.   But yonder look
Where comes another of your fine Court dames.

   Lau. Quick! let us hence!   O father, see you not?
'Tis she—the princess!

   Fab.   She!

   Lau.   Ay, she who rode
By the duke's side in front of all the rest;
I marked her well, and know.   Come, come away.
                                  [*Exeunt.*

   Enter LEONORA, *reading from a scroll.*

   Leo. [*Reading.*] *As the skilled pilot seeks in Nature's
     eyes*
If the wind sleeps, or storms are like to rise,
E'en so in your fair orbs, that light my heaven,
I turn to read what fate to me is given—

And with their changing change, from hope of life
To fear of dying in mine own heart's strife.
And it is true—each word. What woman e'er
Kindled a hotter love in man than this?
More hot with ev'ry day. I must take heed
It flame not out too broadly, so to set
Winking the blear-eyed gossips of the world.
But how now! he himself! Ay, and he marks
His paper in my hand. I must take heed.

Enter TASSO.

So! Signor Tasso! welcome. As you see,
I here am reading those same verses o'er
That last you sent me; they are freighted full
Of sweetest music.
 Tas.   If by you approved,
They find their meed. Do you accept them too?
 Leo. Accept! 'twere strange if I should not accept
A gift so precious. Yet I hope you purpose
To make the world a sharer.
 Tas.   What in them
Is yours, is yours alone. I should have said
Do you accept their meaning? Will your eyes
Deal me out life, or death?
 Leo.   Nay now, so grave?
Who but a poet would so seriously
Accept a poet's meaning?
 Tas.   Pray you think
A poet is a man, with a man's sense

Of heat and cold, of hunger, thirst, and pain—
In brief, with all the feelings that make up
The thing that men call man.
    Leo.   Now on my word
I see you are not well; you shake and burn
As one already caught within the toils
Of some fierce sickness.   I will get you help. [*Going.*
    Tas. [*Overtaking and detaining her.*] Remain; thou
        shalt. O pardon me, nor think
I am aught else than humble still to you,
But heard at last I must be.

Enter FABRIZIO *and* LAURA, *at the back. They see* TASSO *and* LEONORA, *and stand watching them.*

                              You know well
I have been long content much to desire,
Little to hope, and nought to ask; but now
The time is come that I must ask or die.
    Leo. Heed how you speak.
    Tas.   Nay, I must speak, must ask—
Must speak my love that, pent up here, doth shake
And rive its prison-walls, must ask for yours—
Your love—O give me, give!
    [LAURA *covers her eyes with one hand, and gives the other to her father, who leads her away.*
    Leo. [*After a pause.*]   Let me recall
Unto your memory how unfit these words
Are to be said by you, or heard by me.

But since I would be loth the pleasant hours
Of friendship we have known and yet may know
Should all be wrecked by one rash moment's breath,
I will forget I heard, if on your side
You will forget you spoke.

 Tas.   How now ! so cold !
In word, in look, so cold ! But word and look
May bear false witness. No, it cannot be—
I'll not believe—in nature is it not,
Not possible by her law, that what is here
Could to such hugeness grow were nought in thee
Create to answer it. God sent us hunger,
But bade the earth be fruitful—thirst, but stored
The wand'ring clouds with rain ; then must it be
That when so greatly he lets Tasso love,
Leonora loves a little. Speak ! O speak !
            [*Seizing her hand.*

 Leo. Let go my hand. If any should be near !
I say let go. What ! will you not ? Why then,
I must remind you, sir, these vows are due
To another, not to me. In Mantua
You loved a maiden once, and, I have heard,
Gave her your troth ; go back to her, and shame
To be in love so faithless.

 Tas. [*Letting go her hand.*] Faithless—yea—
The word is true, though from your lips 'tis one
I thought not to have heard. And she was good,
And loved me, and would ne'er have taunted me.

Enter a Page.

Page. Here, Signor Tasso, is a ring of yours
That I am bid deliver.
Tas.   What means this?
[*Taking the ring.*] A ring! this ring! who gave it?
  who? who? where?
Page. They told me if you asked I was to say
It mattered not, but that the ring was yours.   [*Exit.*
Tas. Ay, 'tis the same.
Leo. [*Approaching him with curiosity.*] What riddle
  have we here?
Tas. You were pleased, madam, to remind me now
I owed my faith to another.   That was so,
But is no longer; see, she sends it back—
The ring I gave her, that with such sweet light
Of truth outshining from her eyes she took.
And true she was, and good; but now for ever
Her goodness and her truth to me are lost,
Lost, and through thee—through thee, by whom I
  have lost
All that was mine, and mine own self to boot.
Ay, but at least I will not lose thee too;
Thou shalt repay me all.   Think not to 'scape.
              [*Laying hold of her.*
Leo. Fall back, presumptuous.   Back, upon thy life.
Tas. So! now you are the princess? O I know—
You play the woman when you would lead me on,
The princess when 'tis fit to hold me off;

But I—I through it all am still a man,
And not a jointed toy to be wound up
To play in any game what part you please.
I am a man, and love thee with man's love,
And thou must give me love for love, and shalt.

  Leo. Hark! voices! hear you not? Fool, let me go.

  Tas. Not till thou first hast plighted me thy troth—
Thus, thus, and thus.   [*Embracing her.*

Enter DUKE, *with Courtiers and Attendants, among
  them* ASCANIO, FRANCESCO, *and* MADDALO.

  Leo.   Away!
  Duke.   My sister!
   [*On hearing the* DUKE'S *voice,* TASSO *suddenly
    releases her.*

  Leo. [*Rushing up to the* DUKE.]   Help!
He is mad—O save me, brother!

  Duke.   Seize him, sirs—
On your allegiance, seize him.

   [*A short struggle, in which* TASSO *is overpowered.*

  Mad.   Good my lord,
We have him fast.

  Duke.   Then take away his sword.
Nay, nay, no need to handle daintily;
He hath deserved the worst.

  Fran.   The very worst.

  Asc. [*Aside.*] And will not have much better.

  Duke.   And now, slave,
Say, what is this that thou hast dared to do?

Tas. Before I speak, take back that word of slave,
And keep it for thyself, whom nature made
More fit than I to wear it.
    Duke.   Wouldst thou——
    Tas.   Slave
Is not my name, at least not now my name,
For once it was—what time I hired myself
For paltry hire to a paltry hirer, one
Small in all things save appetite of power
And lust of lying praises which I sang—
Not now; now am I free, and stand once more
What I was born, thy better.
    Leo.   Out alas!
I told you he was mad, and now you see.
    Tas. False woman, nay, not mad, and this thou
        knowest.
Thou hast beggared me of all the goods of life,
Hast lured me on to the very edge of hell,
But hast not made me mad.
    Leo.   I have not, no,
For e'en from the beginning wast thou mad
Of thine own vanity. If first thy brain
Had not been turned by that, how couldst thou deem
That I, a princess of great Este's house,
E'er stooped to try my lures on such as thou?
Brother, I pray you make me safe from him
In time to come. You see that he is mad;
As a madman deal with him.
    Tas.   And this is she—

She for whose sake I gave up life and love.
O fool, fool, fool!
 Duke.   Sister, you counsel well.
[*To Attendants.*] To the madhouse at Ferrara take
 him straight.   [*The Curtain falls.*

END OF ACT III.

ACT IV.

SCENE I.

Ferrara. A Room in the Hospital of St. Anna. The joyous chiming of church bells is heard at intervals from without.

SCIPIO GONZAGA *and* ANTONIO COSTANTINI *discovered.*

Sci. Being so near to see him I find now
To see him I well-nigh fear.—Who is't? Nay, only
The warder once again.

Enter a Warder from an inner room.

Will he not come?
War. 'Tis as I thought; he sleeps. He is given much
To those strange ways, like many of them here—
To wake all night, and rest when sane men stir.
Shall I not rouse him up?
Sci.   No, pray you, no;
We have leisure, and with your good leave will wait.
Disturb him would we not.
War.   Hark to the bells!

Now the procession is upon its way—
At foot of the street perchance if I could see.
                    [*Goes to the window.*
Nay, from this bodkin-slit no seeing is—
Too narrow and deep-set.   'Tis hard to stay
Caged behind iron bars when all the world
Is looking at the show.
    Ant.   And hard on others
Within these walls than you.
    War.   Tut, for those others,
They are mad, and have no right to think aught hard.
I have my reason, and I say 'tis hard
I should be kept penned in on such a day,
As though 'twere once a month or once a week
That a duke's heir brings home a fair young bride.
Well, well, I have work to do, and other work
Than only here.   You said that you would wait—
But can belike spare me?
    Sci.   Friend, doubt it not.
    War. Why, that is good.   I have other work than
        here.   [*Exit.*
    Sci. And in such place as this for seven long years,
And in such guardianship as yonder churl's,
The greatest poet of the world hath lived!
    Ant. Ay, in such place, and in such guardianship;
And worse than these at first—in a foul cell
A single stride could measure, and where light
Was just enough to show the noisomeness
And horror all around, where damp-dewed walls,

Not to be pierced by sunshine or by air,
Served not to shut out sounds of maniac yells,
Echoed by idiot laughter, or sometimes
By crack of keeper's whip. Through favour 'twas,
And prayers of many friends, that to these rooms
You seem to shudder at he hath been advanced.

 Sci. Alas! what hath he borne! And how enough
Shall I, his friend, e'er thank you, noble youth,
Who, in this town a dweller, have had power,
Denied to me, to be his comforter,
And have abounded so in willingness
That but by aid of you and your kind cares
Hath much-tried nature held her own so long.

 Ant. Would only that more power were mine to make
This world to him a little easier
To whom I am in debt for the fairest hours
That e'er it had for me. O say, good sir,
You are great among the great, can you not help
The friend you love so well from out this tomb
Where living men lie buried?

 Sci.   For what end
Unless to try to help is't that I come
Unto Ferrara now? And to prevail
I hope at last, for greater ones than I,
Princes and princes' kinsmen of well-nigh
Each court of Italy, and the Pope himself,
Are intercessors with me in this cause.
Against so many and such prayers as these
It cannot be the duke should still hold out.

Ant. Against them all by turns he hath held out
Seven weary years.
   Sci.   But more than ever yet
They are now importunate, and with them join
The bride and bridegroom that come home to-day.
I am bid to-night to that great feast he gives
In honour of their nuptials; when 'tis done,
Then will I make my suit—nor can I think
At such a time of joy but that one sound
Of sorrow by its discord will be heard,
And force at last his pity.
   Ant.   So 'twould be
With any save this duke, but he in hate
Hath shown himself so rich, I needs must fear.
   Sci. His hate hath wreaked itself. And then the
      cause,
Or what they say was cause, of all these ills
Hath, with the Princess Leonora's death,
Been ta'en away, and should be now forgot.
   Ant. Ay, she is dead, but in her brother still
Her spirit lives—and yet so many prayers
Perchance may exorcise it. But I counsel
Of all these strivings to our friend say nought;
He hath hoped so oft in vain, and from the height
Of hope been cast so oft to the hard ground
Of stony desolation, that methinks
Once more to be so raised and so to fall
Would make him in good earnest what the duke,
And duke's physicians, call him.

Sci.   Trust me well ;
He shall hear nought until success is sure.
Peace, peace—he comes. Is't he indeed ?

Enter TASSO *from the inner room.*

                                     My friend !
Look on me, friend. But how ! you know me not !

     Tas. Your servant, sir. My good Antonio,
You are welcome now and ever.

     Sci.   And for me
Have you no word ? Hath Tasso quite forgot
Scipio Gonzaga ?

     Tas. [*To* ANTONIO.] Is it in good sooth
Scipio Gonzaga ?

     Ant.   Ay, most sure.

     Tas. [*To* SCIPIO.]   Your pardon ;
I knew that you were like him, but oft-times
I am deceived by fancies, that put on
Familiar shapes and voices. Since indeed
You are Scipio, you are welcome. How fare all
In Rome ? for 'tis from Rome, I think, you come.

     Sci. Yes, and to see you, friend.

     Tas.   I thank you much.
You look upon me strangely. I'll be sworn
You deem, because I said that I had fancies,
That I am mad—but no, I am not mad,
Though 'tis the will of one in a high place
I should be so. But let me tell you, sir
That living in a madhouse seven years

May well make reason call in self-defence
A fancy now and then unto her aid.
   Sci. Past doubt, past doubt.
   Tas.   But come, for other things.
I am well pleased we meet again, although
When last we parted we thought not that here
Should our next meeting be.
   Sci.   We thought it not;
Nor thought, when time should that next meeting bring,
You would have gathered in so full a harvest
As now is yours of glory. O my friend,
You are rich in sorrow, but in comfort too,
Of such rare sort that some would buy it gladly
With cost of all your pain. You lie in prison,
But from your prison you have given forth
A poem so noble that more eyes are turned
Unto these walls than to the palaces
Whence princes issue words of life and death.
Is there here no amends?
   Tas.   You speak not this
Only to please me, but in sober truth?
By the world is my " Jerusalem " indeed
So well accepted?
   Sci.   And accounted one
'Mong its best treasures, and the name of him
Who hath so enriched mankind is on the wings
Of fame borne forth to earth's remotest bounds,
So that in lands you know not you are known,
And your name held in honour.

Tas.   Yea, my name—
But I myself am here. Unto my griefs
My glories are not equal.
  Sci.   Well I know
Your griefs indeed are great.
  Tas.   O but how great
You know not, nor can know, who ne'er have known
What 'tis to lie and long to be giv'n back,
Not to the rights of men—that were too much—
But those at least of beasts, who make their home
In the hollow of what tree may like them best,
To whom the fountains yield their crystal drink,
The hills their herbage, and on whom unasked
The fair blue heav'n sends down its gladsome light
And breathes its cooling fever-healing breath.
O for one hour of these! No guilty wretch
Was ever so tormented by the rack
As I by longings for the commonest things
That Nature hath, that yet are not for me.
  Sci. Take comfort. Who shall say how near at last
Deliverance may be?
  Tas.   Nay, I have learned
More wisdom than to hope. I used to dream
It must be near, and prayed and pleaded hard
To God and man each hour of day and night;
But now I know that pity is either dead,
Or else by princes banished from the earth,
And fled for refuge to the highest heaven—
Too high to hear; so must I still be left

In this grim place to think and think again,
And, thinking, madden.

Sci. Pray you speak not thus,
To give a triumph to your enemies.

Tas. What! said I 'madden'? 'twas a foolish word.
I am not mad—though seven years lived here
Is a long time. But in good faith to-day
I am not well, and say I scarce know what;
My head is dizzy, and full of jangling sounds
Like church bells ringing. You hear nought of this?

Sci. Nay, who hears not those chimes? They ring
to honour
The duke's young heir, who hath to-day brought home
His new-wed bride.

Tas. So they indeed are real?
I knew it not, for sometimes in mine ears
Bells peal, and music, that none hears save me—
Yea, sometimes to mine eyes strange shapes appear
That no man else may see, and make my soul
Weak like a reed that trembles in the wind.

Sci. Think not too much of these; they are but
dreams.

Tas. O that word dream might surely better fit
The real life that in the past I lived
Than some of those unreal visions now.
But they are not all dreadful; some are fair,
And fill my heart with comfort. One of these
That men would call my dreams hath come so oft,
And seems so real, that I fain must think

'Tis sent to me for sign to help me read
My life aright.
 Sci.   And what is then this dream?
 Tas. One with a fair beginning and fair end,
Though in the middle dismal. First I see
(And though I say a dream, I see it awake)
The Capitol at Rome, prepared and decked
For some great festival, with waiting crowds
Looking one way. And in the midst of all,
Upon a daïs raised, in robes of state
And crowned with triple crown, doth stand the Pope,
Who holds a laurel wreath high o'er the brow
Of one who kneels before him like myself.
But even as the garland on my head
Doth seem descending, a dark figure steals
Across the picture, and with lifted hand
Strikes, and it vanishes, and where it was
Is left a black-draped bier, and, stretched thereon,
A thing like mine own corse, with waxen brow
Bound round with withered leaves. A fearful sight—
But not the worst, for then the figure turns,
And shows——divine me now what face it shows.
 Sci. How should I tell?
 Tas.   Think of my deadliest foe,
And you will know; the slayer of my life,
The fair witch Circe that hath thrust me here
To herd with worse than beasts—and I, poor fool,
Once took her for the genius of my fame,
The fame that she hath murdered. 'Tis her face

That turns, and smiles with a triumphant smile,
Exulting o'er her work.
 Sci.   O never let
A dream so shake you.
 Tas.   But it ends not thus;
I have a guardian spirit left me still.
E'en as she smiles, she feels her conqueror
And my deliverer near, and hides her eyes,
And cowers, and glides away—and on the ground
That she hath yielded comes a second shape,
A woman too in seeming, clad in black,
Save for a veil of blue upon her head
Woven with stars, even as dark-robed night
Crowned with the lights of heaven. In her hand
She bears a laurel branch, at touch whereof
The thing that so hath chilled my blood gives place,
And in its stead a fair bright star shines out
Amid the darkness, circled round with green
Of living laurel—unto me I hope
The token of my soul as it shall be
When ruin hath done its worst.
 Sci.   And so the vision
Here makes its end?
 Tas.   Ay, for she turns away,
And goes back whence she came, I all this time
Not having seen her face, strive as I may;
And this indeed sore troubles me, that yet
I am not counted worthy of the sight
Of my good angel, and know not what likeness

She wears 'mong spirits and men. Sometimes I think
It needs must be the Queen of Heav'n herself
That pities me, for sure no other would
That e'er took shape of woman. Is't not strange
Women are called gentle and soft of heart?
I have not proved them so.
 Sci.   You found one hard;
But judge not all by one.
 Tas.   O I doubt not
That there are best and worst; but best and worst
Are both alike in this, that they must have
From him who loves them sacrifice. The worst
Would have him suffer, that his sufferings
May make them glorious; but e'en the best,
Who care not to be famous in the world,
Would still have something, and require of him
To be for love of them obscure as they.
Yet these, I say, are best, these are the ones
Who truly love, or truly think they love,
And who perchance to him that yielded all
Would give a rich return. No more, no more—
I made my choice for fame, and fame must have,
And fame must work for. Please you stand aside—
Where are my papers? I must work; too long
You keep me idle. [*Taking papers from a drawer,
  and arranging them on a table.*
 Sci.   And what work is this?
 Tas. A poem which my others shall excel
E'en as its theme does theirs, which is indeed

The story of the wondrous week of days
Wherein the world was made. You see this time
The glory of God and not of man I sing;
I am tired of man for patron. [*Sitting down to his
   papers, then pushing them away.*
                        Nay, to write
The day is too far spent—and in this place
They trust their lodgers with no light save heaven's.
But I can think. Disturb me not, I pray.
   Ant. 'Tis bootless more to try to speak with him;
He is rapt, and will not answer.
   Sci.   And in truth
'Tis time that I were hence; it waxes dark,
And the last chimes have died in the evening air.
The hour is come that I must seek the duke
And the duke's feast, e'en for the sake of him
Who makes to me the thought of feasting sad.
[*To* TASSO.] Friend, fare you well; I have outstayed
      my time,
And must be gone.
   Tas. [*Without looking up.*] Farewell.
   Sci.   You will have at least
The moon to light your labours.
                        [*Exit, with* ANTONIO.
   [*The room is now dark, except for the light of
      the moon shining in at the window.*
   Tas.   Yea, the moon—
The lesser light that o'er the night bears rule.
O on that night when first her pallid beams

Began to yellow through the dark'ning sky,
How fair an unspoiled world she must have seen—
Where man was not, nor conscious sense of self
To mar the even balance of the beauty
Prepared for all—where nought was but the sea
And the new earth, the sea with friendly arms
Clasping the green coast softly, and the earth
Smiling at heaven through the tender haze
Of the first spring's young verdure. O such beauty
How shall I rightly paint, I who so long
Have looked upon no prospect but grey walls
And a locked door? yet shall the very hunger
Of mine eyes feed my fancy.
  [*A chiming of bells is heard, but with a fainter
  and more muffled sound than those which rang
  during the earlier part of the scene.*] What! again
Those bells to harass me! He said methinks
That they were marriage-bells—but what have I
With marriage-bells to do? No, no, not thus;
Not for a marriage these—I know their tone—
'Tis for my coronation that they ring,
My triumph at the Capitol. Once more
I shall behold—once more. It comes, it comes.
  [*Gazes at the wall at the back of the stage, which gra-
  dually becomes luminous, and presently shows a
  public place approached by steps, with a palatial
  building in the background and another at each side,
  forming three sides of a square. At the base of the
  steps a large crowd is assembled, and at the top is*

a raised platform, on which kneels a figure like
TASSO, *with the Pope holding a wreath of laurels
over his head.*

O Holy Father, haste; put on the crown—
Now—now—ere any hinder. Nay, too late;
She is here who is my foe.

[*The figure of a woman glides before the picture, and at
a wave of her hand it melts away, and in its place
appears a bier, on which a form lies like that of*
TASSO, *crowned with withered leaves.*

                                   And death is here,
Mine and my glory's death—and yet to me
So hateful not as she by whom 'tis wrought.

[*The figure turns and smiles at him exultingly, showing
the face of* LEONORA.

What! dost thou triumph? Ay, thou hast conquered
    now—
But not for long; another is at hand
Stronger than thou, to whom thou must give place;
In her I put my hope, and thee defy.
But O how long she tarries! Will she fail?
Not so; she comes, I see by thee she comes.

[*The figure of* LEONORA, *as though it saw something
approaching which it feared, lowers its head, and,
hiding its face, glides away, while, from the side
opposite to that by which it leaves, another figure enters,
also of a woman, dressed entirely in black, except for
a blue veil spangled with gold stars, which covers its*

head and face, and holding in its hand a laurel branch. With this it touches the picture of the bier, which disappears, and in its place is seen, on a dark background, a shining star surrounded with a laurel wreath. TASSO *kneels.*

Yea, thou hast come, and with thee to my soul
Brought peace, and healing comfort. But I pray,
Let me once hear thy voice, and see thy face,
Though with the sight I die—for thus meseems
I could die happy, lighted by thine eyes.
How now! thou goest? Nay, a look, one look,
That I may know thee when we meet in heaven.
　　　　　　　　　　[The figure passes out.
Gone—gone—and still unknown. Alone again!
With darkness all alone!
[*Sinks to the ground, where he remains motionless. A pause, during which the star and laurel wreath fade away, leaving the wall as at first.*

　　　　Enter SCIPIO *and* ANTONIO, *with a light.*

Sci.　　　　　　　　Tasso! my friend!
Where art thou? Is this he? O what hath
　　　chanced?
It seems he swoons. Friend! friend!
　Tas.　　　　　　　　Will she not turn?
Not give me one poor look?
　Sci.　　　　　　　What is't thou sayest?
Come, rouse thyself, and hear. I bring good news.

Tas. [*Springing to his feet.*] Good news! that she
    accords my prayer at last?
Where? where? What! only you! You have cheated
    me.
Sci. Yea, only I, but with such news as since
Seven years you have not heard—that you are free.
    Tas. Free! what is that?
    Ant.   To your voice he is not used.
Illustrious Tasso, he hath told you true.
The duke, in honour of the new-wed pair,
And by entreaty from all sides beset,
Hath yielded—you are free.
    Tas. [*Repeating the words mechanically.*] Free! I
    am free.
Sci. Ay, free to seek where in the world you will
The homage you shall find through all the world
Waiting your presence. But now lend your ear,
And of the use to turn your freedom to
I'll give you counsel. As belike you know,
I have in Rome some power, and look ere long
To own yet more, even so much as goes
With the place and title of a Cardinal—
And all my power shall be for you put forth.
Come then to Rome, and there, I pass my word,
You shall be crowned with the poet's laurel crown,
That at the Capitol the Pope's own hand
Shall set upon your head, as once 'twas set
Upon the head of Petrarch.

Tas. [*Clasping his hands with a wild cry.*] Crowned
   at Rome!
At last, at last! I thank thee, Heav'n—at last!
                              [*The Curtain falls.*

END OF ACT IV.

ACT V.

SCENE I.

Rome. A public place, resembling the picture shown in the Fourth Act. On the raised part of the scene, at the top of the steps, a platform is erected, such as that represented in the picture, but unoccupied.

A crowd of Citizens, &c., with Women and Children, discovered at the base of the steps.

An Old Woman. Alack! here's weary waiting.
   1st Cit. As for that,
All waiting's weary. Nought so long keeps broth
From cooling as to blow on't. But indeed
You'll have more waiting; of the appointed time
It still wants much.
   2nd Cit. Ay, the procession yet
Cannot have left the Vatican.
   1st Cit. And e'en
When it hath left, 'twill not be quickly here
Through such thronged ways as lie between—as packed
With starers as a honeycomb with cells.
   Old Woman. The worse for me; my back is like to break.

Had I but known, I'd not have waited thus,
Not to see twenty thousand poets crowned.
 3rd Cit. You will see more than twenty thousand,
  dame.
That were no sight at all; you will see one.
 Old Woman. O sir, I know what thing a poet is
Without your telling. I've a nephew's son
Can reel you off five hundred lines by heart
That this same Signor Tasso made, and ne'er
Stop once to swallow—so I should know, sure.

Enter, at the side, LAURA, *wrapped in a black cloak and hood,* LORENZO *and* CLAUDIA, *making their way through the crowd.*

 4th Cit. What! here are more!
 Loren.   Pray you, a little room.
 4th Cit. Nay, sir, we've stood all day ourselves to
  see,
And cannot now give way.
 Loren.   Let us have space
At least to pass, in courtesy; to be here
Upon this day these ladies have come far.
 4th Cit. So then, pass if you will; but pass behind.
[LORENZO, LAURA, *and* CLAUDIA *come forward to the front of the stage.*
 Loren. [*To* LAURA.] Are you contented thus? or
  shall we seek
To approach yet nearer?
 Lau.   Nay, not nearer; here

We are safe from being known; here will we stay.
    Clau. Why, how you pant for breath! I do but
       hope
You have the strength you think. Look, husband, look;
Seems she not like to faint?
    Lau.   How should you doubt?
Had I not strength, for many a year before
My father died, not once to speak that name?
Yea, e'en to smile, and wear the face of one
Who in her heart was happy? and shall now
My strength not be enough to stand and look?
Trust me; I know myself.
    Clau.   Well, well. And yet
I would you had not come.
    Lau.   Pray grudge me not
This little comfort. I have borne long years
Of sorrow in his sorrow; let me now
Have some taste of his triumph. Do but think,
And say if you would not have travelled far
To see a festival like this to-day
Made for your good Lorenzo?
    Clau.   Ay, in faith—
You know I would. But then he is mine own,
Who loves me, unto whom I am all in all.
    Lau. 'Twas kind, but needless, to remind me thus
Of what was not forgot.—Nay, nay, forgive;
You never dealt me willing stab, I know;
You are good, and I am grateful—and to-day
More grateful than e'er yet, that to my whim

You have yielded, and to this place given me
Your loving escort. Let me count to you
As a sick child, made by some inward hurt
To kindest handling restive.
  Clau.   O poor child!
Would I might heal that hurt!

Enter, from behind, an Officer, who advances to the top of the steps.

  1*st Cit.*   Look, look! at last
Here doth one come in livery of the Pope.
He brings us tidings; now must the procession
Be close at hand.
  2*nd Cit.*   Hush, he would speak.
  Several.   Hush, hush.
  Off. Good friends, his Holiness doth greet you well,
And bids you all depart in quietness
Unto your sev'ral homes; to-day the sight
You wait for will not be.
  Several. [*Murmuring.*] Not be!
  Off.   As much
His Holiness bewails this change as you.
But by unhappy chance that glorious
And all-unrivalled poet, unto whom
The honour of this day was to be done,
The illustrious Signor Tasso, hath been seized
With sudden malady, wherein he now
Lies sick, e'en unto death. Pray get you home.
  1*st Cit.* So this is for our waiting.

Old Woman.   What! no show
To be at all!
    2nd Cit.   If he must needs fall ill,
Was there not yesterday?
    Old Woman.   Or why at least
Should not the Pope have come, and brought the crown?
    Off. Beseech you, friends, give way, and clear the streets.
    1st Cit. Ay, ay, we'll go; at home we are better off.
[*To 2nd Citizen.*] So then farewell, good gossip.
    2nd Cit.   Fare you well.
Here hath been pretty waiting all for nought.
    [*Exeunt Citizens, &c. The Officer, who has stood at the top of the steps, watching the crowd break up, is turning away, when* LAURA *approaches him.*
    Lau. Sir, sir!
    Off.   What would you, madam? By your leave,
I am in haste.
    Lau.   Yet stay to answer this.
Where is he? who is tending him? and how?
With gentle hands, or rough? O marvel not
That I should ask; I used to know him once.
    Off. He is in good keeping, madam, have no fear—
With the holy fathers at the monastery
Of St. Onofrio, whither by his wish
He hath been borne, to have his soul prepared
For Heaven by their pious offices.
    Lau. And are they kind as pious? soft of hand,

And pitying of heart, and skilled in all
A sick man's changing needs?
 Off.   O be at rest.
He for whose welfare you are thus concerned
Is centre of the reverence and care
Of Rome and all Rome's greatest; his close friend,
The Cardinal Gonzaga, is e'en now
In the monastery, watching by his bed.
 Lau. The Cardinal Gonzaga—he that once
Was Scipio Gonzaga called, and kin
To the house of Mantua?
 Off.   Ay, madam, he.
 Lau. I thank you; 'tis enough.
       [*Officer bows, and exit.*
[*To* LORENZO *and* CLAUDIA.] Now come — come
 quick.
 Clau. Why, whither would you go?
 Lau.   Are you so dull?
To the Cardinal Gonzaga, at the monastery
Of St. Onofrio.
 Clau. The Cardinal!
What would you with the Cardinal?
 Lau.   Fear not;
I will not ask him much—only a look,
One little moment's look before I die,
Upon his living face; and that methinks
The Cardinal Gonzaga should not grudge,
Since Scipio Gonzaga 'twas that once
Hurried him from my sight, ere I had time

To impress the image rightly on mine eyes
That in my heart dwells always. Nay, but see,
How do we waste the time! Come, come, make haste.

Clau. But, cousin——

Lau.   Haste, I say.

Loren.   Be't as she will
Our thwarting will not serve; her mind is fixed.

                              [*Exeunt.*

SCENE II.

The Garden of the Monastery of St. Onofrio.

Enter CARDINAL GONZAGA, *with a Physician and a Monk.*

C. Gon. Is this indeed, good doctor, what you say
As your last word—no hope?

Phy.   Ay, even this—
Would I might answer else! But wretched years
Of durance and vain pining so have sapped
And chafed away the outworks of his strength
That now invading sickness finds in him
An undefended fort, that needs must yield
To the first resolved attack.

C. Gon.   O my poor friend!

Monk. And yet have those who love him cause to joy
In his soul's health, more even than to mourn

His body's languishing, for on my word
Not I nor any of my brethren here,
Who have stood by many death-beds, e'er have found
A spirit so devout, or so much zeal
As his to be instructed and prepared
For his great journey.
 Phy.   Ay, 'twould seem already
He counts his mortal life to be at end,
So doth he strive and labour to forget
What to the past belongs, and only think
Of what may lie before. But I must pray
Your Eminence to spare me for a while;
Later I will return, though, as I fear,
My skill can nought avail.
 C. Gon.   Fare you well, doctor.
 Monk. This way, then, sir; I will undo the gate.
      [*Exeunt Physician and Monk.*
 C. Gon. O glorious vessel, in mid-voyage wrecked
Upon a sun-lit sea, when all the storms
Were laid that tore thee! Yet how stately still
Thou seemest, settling down unto thy rest
In the deep silent bosom of all things—
Stately and able still to serve mankind
Well as of old, but for the doom pronounced
That says, it must be. And all this the work
Of one false woman!

Re-enter Monk.

Monk.   Please you, at the gate
There is but just arrived a cavalier
Squiring two ladies, who as earnestly
As though a life upon the issue hung
Beg for brief audience of your Eminence.
  C. Gon. Of me! What would they have?
  Monk.   I know not, sir;
But as I turned to bring to you their prayer,
One of the ladies, who had yet spoke nought,
Said, 'Tell the Cardinal that in the name
Of the Tasso whom he knew in Mantua
I pray this suit be not by him denied.'
  C. Gon. Ay, said she so? Go bring them hither,
    friend;
That name shall be their passport.   [*Exit Monk.*

Enter LORENZO, LAURA, *and* CLAUDIA.

                   Which is she
That in the name of Tasso made her suit?
  Lau. 'Twas I, lord Cardinal. You know me not?
But 'tis no marvel; though I know you well,
Nor is that marvel either, for the day
That first and last I saw you was that day
When last on me he looked, that day you came
And 'twixt us twain made parting.
  C. Gon.   She! O lady,
Albeit I was so slow to know you now,

Forgot you have I not—nay, but full oft
Have thought on you and on your grief that day,
Sometimes well-nigh repenting of the share
I had in causing it.
 Lau.   You now may make
Amends, if so you will.
 C. Gon.   O show me how;
Trust me, I would do much.
 Lau.   For tedious years
That since that day have passed, my soul hath lived
On memories of his voice and of his face,
That from each weary waking fill my thoughts
Until the wearier lying down to sleep.
But lately hath a hunger in me grown
To add to these one other memory more,
Were't only of a moment—such a hunger
That till 'tis satisfied the pain of it
Gives me no leave to rest, or e'en to die.
For this I came to Rome, in hope to stand
In the throng far off, and watch him being crowned.
Crowned now I may not see him, but at least
May look upon him dying, if so be
That you deny me not.
 C. Gon.   Nor would I, lady,
But for his sake. You have not thought how much
Your presence might disturb the dying hours
That 'tis your wish to soothe.
 Lau.   Have I so ill
Interpreted myself that to my wish

You attribute such presumption? O no, no,
Not to be seen by him, or speak with him,
My craving is; he loves me not enough
To give me so much right; all that I would
Is but to look upon his face once more
Far off, for one brief instant, he the while
Of me nought thinking—and you need not fear
That though the sight should move me in my soul
  Twould bring from me a sound that he could hear.
I well am used to curb myself, and know
That I can bear in silence.   Then I pray,
Let not your doubts debar me from the thing
I only prize—but trust me.

   C. Gon.   And I do—
I do, and will.   In his presence you shall stand,
And see his face, so you are but content
To look upon him sleeping, and to wait
Till sleep shall come to him.

   Lau.   Sir, my last prayer,
Save one, shall be that Heav'n may make you bless'd
For this good deed.   And now I have still a boon
To ask you for, but this so small that sure
'Twill easily be granted.

   C. Gon.   And what is't?

   Lau. My lord, as in this garden I set foot,
I saw, hard by the gate, a laurel grow—
A fair and stately plant—and to my mind
There came a fancy that 'twould do me good,

And good perchance to him, if I might lay
A branch thereof beside him on his bed.
He used to say the laurel was my tree,
And I would fain that something that is mine
Might at the last lie near him.   May this be?
   C. Gon. Surely it may; this boon is small indeed.
   Lau. Beseech you, good Lorenzo, bring me hither
A branch of that same laurel.   [*Exit* LORENZO.
                               And meantime,
Sweet cousin, of your kindness give me help
To muffle so myself that if he woke,
And saw, he should not know me.   Draw my hood
Down on my brow—nay, more.   'Tis not enough;
I should have had a veil.   O look—your scarf—
Lend me; 'twill serve.   Cast it about my head.
[CLAUDIA *throws her scarf, of blue gauze, spangled with
    stars, over* LAURA'S *head, in such a manner that
    the latter, being already dressed in black, is rendered
    an exact counterpart of the second female figure of*
    TASSO'S *vision in the Fourth Act.*
Ay, now 'tis right; I thank you.

     Re-enter LORENZO, *with a laurel branch.*

   Loren.   Cousin, here
I bring what you would have.
   Lau. [*Taking the branch.*]   A living branch
Of the tree he loves—or loved.
   C. Gon.   You are ready now?
Why then, come all within, and there await

The fitting moment that to one of you
Shall give the promised sight so much desired.
                                    [*Exeunt.*

SCENE III.

A Room in the Monastery.

TASSO *discovered on a bed, sitting supported by pillows, and surrounded by the Monks of St. Onofrio and their Prior, the Monks chanting a hymn, to which he listens with hands folded in prayer.*

HYMN.

Soli tibi, Domine,
Fides nostra tribuatur;
Solus tu laudabilis,
Solus tu amabilis;
Fides nostra tribuatur
Soli tibi, Domine.

Tecum solo, Domine,
Vita floret sempiterna;
Omnis mundi gloria
Languet, et victoria;
Vita floret sempiterna
Tecum solo, Domine.

Tas. [*the hymn being finished.*] And to Thee only
do I look—Thee only—
Thou see'st that this is so. For O 'tis sure,

In Him alone is life that lives indeed,
In Him true immortality.   The world,
And glory of the world, is vain and slight—
Not worth the seeking.   You are well assured
Of this, even as I?
 Prior.   We know it, son.
 Tas. I know it too; I said, and say again,
Not worth the seeking—and belike, if had,
Not worth the keeping.   Glory is of earth,
And all the things of earth have once been dust,
And must be dust again; what should it serve
To have filched a handful more than other men
Of powdered rottenness?   For me, no longer
I reck of glory, and have only Heaven
For my ambition now.
 Prior.   And e'en herein
Hath Heaven shown its favour to thee, son,
Putting this new ambition in thy heart,
So gracious in its manner and its end—
One to all others most unlike in this,
That it makes happy, peaceful, and content,
As in this hour thou provest.
 Tas.   Happy!—Yea,
Happy—no doubt I am happy.   But 'twas time;
I have had long to wait, much to endure.
A hard life, father, mine hath been, all told.
 Prior. Alas! too well I know.
 Tas.   So dost thou say;
But thou know'st not—not thou nor any here.

How should you, peaceful men fenced from the world
And wounds of worldly battle? holy men,
By vows made safe from women—ay, therein
Your great exemption lies—how should you know
What evil may be wrought upon a man
By a woman, a false woman? Look on me,
If you would learn how much.
 Prior.   Nay, nay, I pray,
Feed not your thoughts with such unwholesome food.
 Tas. If not with that, with what? I have no mem'ries
But those that she hath made me, of a life
Ruined and slain by her. Ay, thou false witch,
I say by thee, who like a shadow stealest
Across my glory, shrivelling it up
Into abhorred corruption. It was here,
Was well-nigh on my head, and now is gone,
Blighted by thee. O who will give me back
My glory—my lost glory?
 Prior.   What! again
On earthly glory do thy thoughts decline?
I deemed thou now hadst found a higher care.
 Tas. O pardon; that is so. I had forgot;
I will remember better. Yet 'tis strange
How true it is what I have somewhere read,
That ever is ambition the last garment
Whereof the wise man strips himself. But now
'Tis off—'tis wholly off.

Prior. So much the sooner
Wilt thou achieve Heav'n's glory, as thou most
Despisest that of earth.
Tas. I do despise—
Believe me, Heaven. Nay, I'll bring a proof.
Prior, you know that I have tendered always
My writings as my children, unto me
No children else being given. Burn them, burn.
Is that enough?
Prior. Beseech you, be more calm.
Tas. Make it your work to seek them through the world,
Where'er men read them—burn them all, I say,
And leave not one behind.
Prior. Thou ravest, son.
Tas. I know the task is hard, since they so far
Are spread and multiplied, but if you fail
The fault will not be mine; you see I am willing,
And Heaven sees I am willing, and will sure
Be reconciled at last, and give me rest—
A little rest, for I am sore in need.
So tired I yet was never.
Prior. You are tired
With bootless self-disturbings. Lie you down,
And give yourself some quiet.
Tas. You say right;
I cannot hold out longer. Take away
Some of these pillows—so. Ay, that is well.
It may be I shall sleep, for now I feel

I am of Heav'n accepted. Give me music; [*Solemn music.*
How good to hear sweet music! [*Sleeps, the music still continuing.*

Enter CARDINAL GONZAGA.

C. Gon.   Say, what news?
How doth he fare?
Prior.   Your Eminence, at last
Methinks he sleeps, tired out by restlessness.
   C. Gon. Sleeps! this suits well. Good fathers, whatsoe'er
I now may do, look on, and question not.
I have made a promise which I needs must keep.
                    [*Goes to the door and beckons.*
Approach; the time is come.

Enter LAURA, *veiled as at the end of the previous scene, the laurel branch in her hand. She approaches the bed on which* TASSO *lies, and is about to lay down the branch, when he suddenly awakes and starts up.*

   Tas.   Who's there? What! thou!
Thou—in this room—'mong shapes of flesh and blood,
And real faces—thou! [LAURA *retreats, and is about to leave the room.*] Stay, stay! Nay, stay!
What! wilt forsake me even when I die?
I am dying; may I not have first one look—
One look of that which Heav'n appointed me

For my good angel?

   Lau. [*Tearing off her veil.*] Ha! thou know'st me
     then!
Thou know'st me, my Torquato!
   Tas.   Laura! Thou!
My guardian spirit and good angel, thou!
And yet might I have known. But now I know.
Unto my heart! come! come! [*Holding out his
    arms; she rushes into them.*] O had but eyes
Been given to me earlier—the eyes
Wherewith at last I see! Far, far, my love,
I have wandered since I left thee, and been bruised
By many a batt'ring storm, but now once more
Am safe in port, and to thine arms come home,
Within thine arms to die. Yet O blind fool,
Blind fool that I have been!
                 [*A sound of knocking is heard.*
   A Voice without.   Make open, ho!
Make open, in his Holiness's name.

A Monk opens the door, and Enter the Pope's Chamberlain, followed by Attendants, one of whom carries a cushion with a laurel crown resting on it.

   Cham. God's blessing be with all! His Holiness
Sends us to set the laurel on the brow
Of him whose wearing more will honour it
Than it hath honoured others in time past—
The glorious poet Tasso.

Tas.   O see there!
Now, e'en in this first moment of my life
That nought I care for it, unsought it comes!
And sooner might have come if always thus
I had been content to heed it not, and make
My strivings for the prize of happy love,
That now I see alone worth striving for.
Who seeks but glory can but glory get,
Since better things must for themselves be wooed;
But unto him who seeks those better things
She, being meretricious, oft may throw
Unasked her favour. Thus it might have been
With me if I had known. But now—at last—
Thou hast taught me now, my Laura.
[*After a pause, turning to the Chamberlain.*] Sir,
      declare
Unto his Holiness my thanks, but say
I have already found my laurel crown,
And wear it on my heart. Love, nearer yet;
I am weak, and cannot clasp thee close enough—
Ay, on my heart—my laurel on my heart—
Here on my heart—'tis so.   [*Dies.*

   Prior. [*To Chamberlain.*] Alas! too late
You were sent upon your errand; he is gone
Where honours cannot reach him.
   Cham.   But the Pope
Commanded that if e'en we found him lie
In death already, we should nathless set
This sign of earthly glory on his head

And of the favour of his Holiness.
    [*Approaches the bed with his Attendants.*
Lau. [*Looking up suddenly.*] What would you? Ay,
    is't so? O have your way;
Put on his brow the laurel if you will
But dare not seek to take it from his heart,
For there it lives, and thence shall never part.
    [*Sinks down embracing* TASSO's *body. The laurel i
    placed on his head by the Chamberlain, and the
    Curtain falls.*

THE END.

LONDON:
Printed by JOHN STRANGEWAYS, Castle St. Leicester Sq.

BY THE SAME AUTHOR.

LADY JANE GREY.
INEZ; or, The Bride of Portugal.

Opinions of the Press.

PALL MALL GAZETTE (*Jan.* 19, 1872).

'These two tragedies possess the features which are essential, as Mr. Arnold has pointed out, to really fine poetry. In both the action is noble, the expression beautiful and consistent; in both the reader will be less struck by isolated passages, remarkable though many of these are, than by the congruity of the whole. In the simple mode of telling his story Mr. Ross Neil resembles a careful chronicler; in the distinctness of the characters he shows his skill as a dramatist; and throughout his tragedies the play of a carefully regulated imagination marks the dominant faculty of the poet. Mr. Ross Neil is not the first dramatist who has chosen Lady Jane Grey's misfortunes as the subject for a tragedy; but it may be safely said that he alone has done justice to the theme.'

SATURDAY REVIEW (*Dec.* 16, 1871).

'If the choice of really dramatic subject-matter, and a treatment as sound and delicate as it is completely free from affectation, are worth appreciation, these two plays deserve a sincere welcome. . . . A composition of remarkable merit and strength. . . . The author's method is so simple and self-contained as to suggest the pure severity of Greek drama.'

ATHENÆUM (*Dec.* 30, 1871).

'Superior to anything that has lately appeared in the shape of dramatic literature.'

DAILY NEWS (*March* 23, 1872).

'For the first time the beautiful character of Lady Jane Grey may be said to have found a competent poetical interpreter.'

By the same Author.

THE CID.
THE KING AND THE ANGEL.
DUKE FOR A DAY; or, The Tailor of Brussels.

SATURDAY REVIEW (*May* 9, 1874).

'The three plays which are contained in this volume are marked by the same qualities of vigorous simplicity and artistic finish which distinguished Mr. Ross Neil's earlier efforts. . . . Will be read with pleasure by all who can appreciate tender and elevated poetry, as well as by those who relish the vividness of dramatic recital. We should be glad to make the acquaintance of some of his works on the scene on which they are, if not intended, at least well fitted to be produced. . . . The severe historical simplicity of "Lady Jane Grey" would, with capable performers, be extremely impressive on the stage; but possibly such a piece as "The Cid," which contains strong situations and is full of variety and movement, would be more certain of commanding immediate favour.'

SPECTATOR (*July* 25, 1874).

'If it were possible, as has been frequently proposed, to have one theatre in London for the sole representation of the poetical drama, and if this idea, so fruitful in suggestion, could be carried out satisfactorily by actors who were proud of their calling, and before a sympathetic audience, Mr. Neil's dramas would be received, we think, with the approval they merit. Of the three plays before us, the first appears eminently fitted for the stage, or rather for what the stage was in the days of Mrs. Siddons and John Kemble.'

PALL MALL GAZETTE (*Nov.* 17, 1874).

'The artistic qualities manifest in Mr. Neil's tragedies, "Lady Jane Grey" and "Inez," are equally evident in "The Cid." . . . The skill exhibited in the construction of the plot is striking, and the play is generally free from those occasional marks of weakness which destroy the symmetry of so many otherwise fine productions.'

SCOTSMAN (*July* 17, 1874).

'It is difficult in reading these plays to say which the reader will most admire, the exquisite sweetness of the poetry, or the strength of their dramatic character. . . . They could scarcely fail, if put upon the stage, to give as much pleasure to those who witnessed them as they will to every one who may read them. . . . The third play, "Duke for a Day," is intensely humorous, and it is also managed with infinite skill and elegance.'

By the same Author.

ELFINELLA; or, Home from Fairyland.
LORD AND LADY RUSSELL.

ATHENÆUM (*July* 29, 1876).

'It ["Elfinella"] is very refined, elegant, and fanciful in treatment, and displays much poetic taste and culture. . . . In dealing with Lord and Lady Russell, Mr. Ross Neil has supplied a striking picture of the court of the second Charles. . . . Mr. Ross Neil's work is admirably firm and conscientious, and his drama will maintain a place in literature.'

SATURDAY REVIEW (*April* 29, 1876).

'This bare outline, however, gives a very insufficient idea of the graceful mingling of humour and tenderness with which the joyous but idle sportiveness of Fairyland is contrasted with the deep and serious experiences of human life. . . . A natural and suggestive study of character, in which even the fairies are felt to be at home. . . . . Plays of this kind ["Lord and Lady Russell"], dealing with subjects of national interest, and in a tone which excites sympathy with the noblest emotions, might do much in making public opinion not only more refined and intellectual, but more robust.'

WESTMINSTER REVIEW (*July*, 1876).

'Mr. Neil's "Elfinella; or, Home from Fairyland," breathes the same spirit as the "Midsummer Night's Dream," or "The Faithful Shepherdess," or "The Sad Shepherd."'

LONDON QUARTERLY REVIEW (*Oct.* 1876).

'The subject [of "Elfinella"] is most gracefully wound through the four acts of the drama, and the conclusion is eminently satisfactory. "Lord and Lady Russell," though painful as any drama on such a subject must be, is full of genuine pathos, and strong in human interest throughout. . . . . We can imagine that many would select "Lord and Lady Russell" as Ross Neil's masterpiece.'

TIMES (*December* 1, 1876).

'We have read with pleasure several of Mr. Ross Neil's earlier dramas—"Inez," "Duke for a Day," "Lady Jane Grey," and "The Cid." But as "Elfinella" has been actually submitted to the practical test of the stage, we prefer to single that out for notice. . . . . While the gentle flow of domestic interest seizes on our sympathy from the first, and carries it along to the end, the author has concentrated his energies on certain effective situations, to which everything else is carefully subordinated. The emotions excited by the action under thrilling circumstances of the most exalted passions in our nature are relieved by a lively play of fancy.'

PALL MALL GAZETTE (*May* 1, 1877).

'We have left ourselves no space for any adequate criticism of "Lord and Lady Russell;" but we regret this the less since on previous occasions we have given our impression of Mr. Neil's merit as an historical dramatist. The play is admirably conceived, and the execution is worthy of the conception.'

SCOTSMAN (*April* 21, 1876).

'The volumes which Mr. Neil has already published have gained the good opinion of those who could understand what real poetry was, and how much more powerful it may often be made when poetic genius is allied with dramatic instinct. . . . It ["Elfinella"] is in truth one of the most interesting of Mr. Neil's plays, because, perhaps, it is the most fanciful. . . . The treatment of the story ["Lord and Lady Russell"] is suggestive and eminently artistic throughout. . . . There is not a touch in the whole piece that is not highly dramatic.'

TEMPLE BAR (*January*, 1878).

'We have lingered too long over "Inez" to be able to say much of the other plays. "The Cid," however, it may be said, has the same qualities of dramatic fire and strength that belong to "Inez," and is, as it stands, better suited for stage performance. "Duke for a Day" reveals unexpected traits of keen and unforced humour and satire. . . . Our object has been to point out that the art of dramatic poetry in England is not so destitute of new life as it is sometimes said to be.'

LONDON:
ELLIS & WHITE, 29 NEW BOND STREET.

www.ingramcontent.com/pod-product-compliance
Lightning Source LLC
Chambersburg PA
CBHW030016240426
43672CB00007B/980